A2 Psychology
UNIT 5

AQA

Specification

Module 5: Individual Differences

Mike Ca‎nagan

Philip Allan Updates
Market Place
Deddington
Oxfordshire
OX15 0SE

tel: 01869 338652
fax: 01869 337590
e-mail: sales@philipallan.co.uk
www.philipallan.co.uk

ISBN-13: 978-0-86003-683-8
ISBN-10: 0-86003-683-9

This Guide has been written specifically to support students preparing for the AQA Specification A A2 Psychology Unit 5 examination. The content has been neither approved nor endorsed by AQA and remains the sole responsibility of the author.

Printed by MPG Books, Bodmin

Contents

Introduction

■ ■ ■

Content Guidance

■ ■ ■

Questions and Answers

Introduction

About this guide

This is a guide to the Individual Differences section of AQA(A) A2 Psychology Unit 5, which examines the content of **Module 5: Individual Differences and Perspectives**. It is intended as a revision *aid*, rather than a textbook or revision guide. Therefore, the emphasis is on how the specification content is examined and on showing you how different levels of answer to sample questions will be assessed.

This guide includes the following elements:
- the specification content for each topic. This is explained fully so that you know exactly what you might be asked to demonstrate in an examination.
- appropriate content relevant to each topic. This gives you a minimal coverage of each topic and also guidance on possible synoptic material that might be used in an examination answer. This is not intended as the *only* appropriate content for a given topic area, but it does give you an idea of how you might present your answer to a question set on this particular part of the specification.
- for each topic, a sample question in the style of A2 examination questions, together with a full explanation of its requirements.
- a typical student response to each of these questions, together with examiner comments showing where the marks have been gained and lost.

How to use this guide

This book is not intended as a set of model answers to examination questions, nor as an account of the *right* material to include should you be asked to display this very same knowledge. It is intended to give you an idea of the way that your examination will be structured and how you might improve your own examination performance.

The examination

Structure of the examination

Unit 5 is assessed in a 2-hour examination. The paper will comprise three sections: Section A (Individual Differences), Section B (Perspectives — Issues and Debates) and Section C (Perspectives — Approaches). You are required to select one question from each of these three sections, giving a total of *three* questions to be answered in 2 hours.

Each question is worth 30 marks. Within the Individual Differences section, there will be three questions, one from each 'subsection' of the specification. These are:
- Issues in the classification and diagnosis of psychological abnormality
- Psychopathology
- Treating mental disorders

You are guaranteed one question from each of these three subsections, and you are required to pick *one* of these to answer. This is helpful when it comes to revision (in fact, you will probably only have covered two, or even one, of these subsections in class). It is important to remember, however, that you must revise *everything* in your chosen subsection(s), as you can be assessed on all aspects of it.

AO1 and AO2 skills

Each question will assess your skills in two different areas (known as assessment objectives).

AO1: knowledge and understanding
Examiners look for the following when assessing AO1:
- psychological knowledge. Do you avoid common-sense or anecdotal material?
- understanding. Do you appear to understand what you are talking about?
- construction of the answer. Do you communicate a sound grasp of knowledge and use it to good effect?
- coherence of explanations. Do the sentences make sense? Is there clarity of expression?
- breadth and depth. Have you avoided a 'shopping list' approach? High marks are awarded where a balance between breadth and depth is achieved.

AO2: analysis and evaluation
Examiners look for the following when assessing AO2:
- commentary. Commenting upon the nature of the research is a means of establishing its value (evaluation).
- negative criticism. What flaws are there in the theoretical arguments presented as AO1? If empirical research was described, what methodological faults are there in the study/studies? What mismatch is there with real life?
- positive criticism. What support is there in terms of empirical studies, other theories and/or successful applications?
- interpretation. What conclusions can we draw from the descriptive material? (You might use sentences that start with 'Therefore...', 'So...' or 'This means that...')
- effective use of material. Has the material been used effectively? Ensure that you explain the point being made. Have you explained how the points raised relate to each other?
- appropriate selection. Is the answer clearly directed at the question set rather than a generalised essay on the topic area, or a prepared answer?
- coherent elaboration. You must state the criticism/comment and then *explain* it.

How are the marks awarded?

Mark allocations for Unit 5 questions

AO1 mark allocation

Marks	Content	Detail and accuracy	Organisation and structure	Breadth and depth of content and synoptic possibilities
15–13	Substantial	Accurate and well-detailed	Coherent	Substantial evidence of both
12–10	Slightly limited	Accurate and reasonably detailed	Coherent	Evidence of both
9–7	Limited	Generally accurate and reasonably detailed	Reasonably constructed	Some evidence of both
6–4	Basic	Lacking detail	Sometimes focused	Little evidence
3–0	Just discernible	Weak/muddled/ inaccurate	Wholly/mainly irrelevant	Little or no evidence

AO2 mark allocation

Marks	Evaluation	Selection and elaboration	Use of materials and synoptic possibilities
15–13	Thorough	Appropriate selection and coherent elaboration	Highly effective
12–10	Slightly limited	Appropriate selection and elaboration	Effective
9–7	Limited	Reasonable elaboration	Reasonably effective
6–4	Basic	Some evidence of elaboration	Restricted
3–0	Weak, muddled and incomplete	Wholly or mainly irrelevant	Not effective

Content
Guidance

In this section, guidance is offered on the three subsections of **Individual Differences**.

Each subsection begins with an outline and explanation of the specification requirements. This is followed by a more detailed look at the theories and studies that make up the module content.

Each subsection ends with a synoptic overview. This makes suggestions about how to add a synoptic dimension to your answers.

Names and publication dates have been given when referring to research studies. The full references for these studies should be available in textbooks should you wish to research the topic further.

Classification and diagnosis of psychological abnormality

Classificatory systems

Specification content

Current versions of ICD *and* DSM *as alternative approaches to the classification of psychological abnormality, including research into the reliability and validity of classification and diagnosis (e.g. Rosenhan).*

The backbone of this subsection of the specification is knowledge about the two most widely used classification schemes: *ICD* and *DSM*. You must be able to describe the content of both of these. However, at most you will have only 20 minutes in which to do this, so it is advisable to work out the best way of describing each classification scheme without trying to list all the contents. It may be useful to prepare a 20-minute version and a 10-minute version, and even a 5-minute version. Producing précis in this way helps you to focus on the most essential characteristics.

The specification requires you to be familiar with the most recent version of each scheme. *ICD* is in its tenth revision. The most recent form of *DSM* is *DSM-IV-TR*, a text revision of *DSM-IV* which includes new research information gathered since 1994.

The specification also refers to *ICD* and *DSM* as 'alternatives', which signals the possibility that you might be asked to compare and contrast these two classification schemes. Practice at doing this will be useful in furthering your overall understanding of both schemes.

You may be asked a question specifically on reliability and validity, as these concepts are included in the specification. The term 'research' refers to either theory or studies. For theoretical material, you might consider the different ways that reliability and validity are assessed, and then look at studies that investigate the reliability and validity of the two classification schemes or that investigate classification in general (one such study is given as an example in the specification — Rosenhan's classic study 'on being sane in insane places').

Classification and diagnosis are both mentioned in the specification. The process of classification involves identifying a patient's symptoms. A clinician then hopes to be able to perceive a pattern of symptoms common to a certain disorder and this produces a diagnosis. Classification and diagnosis are part of the same process.

You are required to produce a synoptic response, so some suggestions to help you with this task are included at the end of this topic (see p. 13). Questions will be designed to facilitate this.

Classificatory schemes

	ICD-10 (1992)	DSM-IV (1994) DSM-IV-TR (2000)
Full title	International Statistical Classification of Diseases and Related Health Problems	Diagnostic and Statistical Manual of Mental Disorders
Publisher	WHO (World Health Organization)	APA (American Psychiatric Association)
Aims	To collect data about physical and psychological diseases and related health problems; to compile statistics	To identify clusters of symptoms and match to clinical characteristics of mental disorders
Basis of classification scheme	Some recognition of possible causes, e.g. organic disorders	No assumption about causes; categories are entirely descriptive
Usage	Europe; internationally	USA and Canada
Number of categories	Eleven, including schizophrenia, mood disorders and disorders due to psychoactive substance abuse	Sixteen, including schizophrenia and other psychotic disorders, mood disorders and substance-related disorders
Classification scheme	• Patient assigned to one of 11 categories • Each category is distinguished by a set of descriptive characteristics of the disorder • Within the categories, information on causes (aetiology) is included to satisfy clinicians' desire for such information	Multi-axial system permits a more complete picture of patient: • AXIS I — clinical syndromes • AXIS II — mental retardation/ personality disorders • AXIS III — medical conditions • AXIS IV — current stressors • AXIS V — level of functioning No information on causes involved in making a diagnosis
Some differences in categories	• Organic disorders (e.g. Alzheimer's) and mental retardation are two categories • Dissociative disorders included with anxiety disorders in 'neurotic, stress-related and somatoform disorders' • Sleep and eating disorders in one category of 'behavioural disturbances associated with physiological disturbances and physical factors'	• Organic disorders and mental retardation included in Axis II or III rather than Axis I • Dissociative disorders and anxiety disorders in separate category • Sleep disorders classified separately from eating disorders • Includes reference to culture-bound syndromes in an appendix
Common approach to diagnosis	A few core symptoms (clinical characteristics) are identified, leading to the diagnosis of a syndrome; usually, other symptoms are also present for a reasonable period of time	
Other similarities	Both are related to the medical model of abnormality, based on the idea of symptoms leading to classification of syndromes, then to a diagnosis and, finally, suitable treatment	

	ICD-10 (1992)	*DSM-IV (1994) DSM-IV-TR (2000)*
Reliability (see below for a general discussion of reliability)	• *ICD-10* is claimed to show good reliability • However, Nilsson et al. (1999) reported low inter-rater reliability (just under 60% agreement)	• Early studies of *DSM* found low inter-rater reliability (e.g. Ash 1949) and low test–retest reliability (e.g. Beck 1962) • Much of this unreliability was claimed to be due to lack of clarity over which symptoms belong to which categories • Recent revisions of *DSM* have improved this
Validity (see below for a general discussion of validity)	• High aetiological validity • Information about causes included	• Low aetiological validity: provides no information about causes • Low descriptive validity: multiple diagnoses are very common • Low predictive validity: no information about treatment and prognosis • Not an operational system (tells you what to assess but not how to assess it)

Commentary on classification and diagnosis

Strengths

- *ICD* and *DSM* are continually updated.
- The future course of a problem can be predicted, treatment strategies can be determined, and accurate research can be conducted on the causes and treatment of the disorder.

Limitations

- Reliability: identification of symptoms of mental illness is often subjective, as medical tests cannot be used for diagnosis. However, Falek and Moser (1975) found that inter-doctor reliability when diagnosing physical disorders such as tonsillitis (without using laboratory tests) was no better than for schizophrenia.
- Cultural bias: categories are often dictated by social or political views. Homosexuality was included in earlier revisions and sexual disorders are still covered; this may reflect cultural views. Culture-bound syndromes are not represented fully.
- Gender bias: symptoms lead to overdiagnosis of certain conditions in men or women. For example, a female is more likely to be rated as histrionic than a male (Hamilton et al. 1986).
- Ethical issues: diagnosis leads to **labelling**. For example, an individual becomes an anorexic rather than a person who has anorexia. Labels may be self-fulfilling and lead to disorders being seen as discrete categories.

There are alternative schemes, which rely upon:

- a different cultural basis — the *Chinese Classification of Mental Disorders* (*CCMD-2-R*, 1995) contains 10 categories fairly similar to *ICD*. It includes cultural-distinctive categories and excludes behaviours not found in China, such as pathological gambling.
- a different model of abnormality — a behavioural classification scheme was developed by Goldfried and Davison (1976). It includes categories such as deficient behavioural repertoires and aversive self-reinforcing systems to enable classifications in terms of observable and maladaptive behaviours.
- a different approach — *DSM* and *ICD* are **nomothetic** systems, based on generalisations about people. Some clinicians use a more **idiographic** approach where each patient is treated as a unique case. This approach makes it hard to develop an understanding of the causes of mental disorder.

Problems with the classification of mental disorders

Reliability

A diagnosis should be the same (consistent) when repeated. This can be demonstrated by:

- **inter-rater reliability** — comparing diagnoses made by two or more clinicians
- **test–retest reliability** — where the same clinician assesses the same information at different times

Reliability can be improved by training and by using computer programs and standardised interview schedules, which increase objectivity. Some diagnostic criteria remain subjective, for example comparison with an 'average person' (criterion for mania). Reliability has improved with recent revisions of *ICD* and *DSM*.

Validity

Validity concerns whether a person has been given the 'right' diagnosis, and whether classificatory systems measure what they claim to measure. This can be established through:

- **aetiological validity** — the disorder has the same cause in all patients who have the disorder (aetiology = cause)
- **descriptive validity** — patients in different diagnostic categories should differ from each other
- **predictive validity** — diagnosis should lead to a predictable course of disease and outcome of treatment

Descriptive validity is reduced by **comorbidity**. Patients often have two or more disorders; for example, a patient with anorexia often has symptoms of depression too. The increasing success of therapies demonstrates predictive validity. Validity is related to reliability, as illustrated in Rosenhan's classic study.

On being sane in insane places (Rosenhan, 1973)

Eight pseudopatients, presenting only one symptom (hearing voices), sought treatment in several mental hospitals. Seven were diagnosed as being schizophrenic and all eight were admitted. In hospital, 'normal' behaviours were viewed as abnormal by the staff, confirming the diagnosis. Eventually, the pseudopatients were released, with the diagnosis 'schizophrenia in remission'.

A follow-up study warned hospitals that pseudopatients would be seeking diagnosis. No pseudopatients were actually involved, but 41 real patients were judged by at least one clinician to be pseudopatients.

Both studies indicate a lack of reliability and validity in diagnosis. However, these studies used less reliable classificatory schemes than are used now. In addition, the studies lacked validity because it is unrealistic for individuals to describe themselves as insane when they are not. This led clinicians to err on the side of caution and produce a diagnosis of schizophrenia. In the second study, clinicians, having been told of the previous study, were more cautious because they did not want to look foolish.

Synoptic overview

Different explanations or perspectives

ICD and *DSM* represent two different approaches to the classification of mental disorders. There are other approaches that relate to different cultures or models.

Demonstrating different methods used

Information about mental disorders is collected from **case histories**. Statistical data are analysed in **epidemiological studies** (the study of incidence and distribution of diseases).

Relating overarching issues and debates

- **Cultural** and **gender bias** — these are inherent in the schemes.
- **Reductionism** — this is a characteristic of classificatory schemes.

Links with other areas of the specification and other disciplines

- **AS abnormality** — classification and diagnosis of eating disorders, medical versus behavioural model.
- **Psychopathology** — classification and diagnosis of schizophrenia, depression and anxiety disorders.
- **Treating mental disorders** — means of demonstrating predictive validity.

Broad issues of psychological concern

- **Reliability** and **validity** — classification schemes strive to be high in both.
- **Nomothetic versus idiographic** — some classification schemes aim to be more individual-based.
- **Labelling** — this raises ethical problems.

Multiple-personality disorder (dissociative identity disorder)

Specification content

Case studies of multiple-personality disorder (e.g. Thigpen and Cleckley). Research into multiple-personality disorder as a spontaneous or iatrogenic (manufactured by the therapist) phenomenon.

Multiple-personality disorder (MPD) is the term that has been used for many years when referring to this disorder. However, this was changed in a recent revision of *DSM* to 'dissociative identity disorder' (DID), which explains why both terms are given in the specification.

In general, MPD is studied by looking at case studies of individuals diagnosed with the disorder. This is mainly because the disorder is relatively rare. There are a number of well-known case studies, such as the study of 'Eve' by Thigpen and Cleckley (1954). Other case studies are discussed below.

You should be able to describe and evaluate these case studies. One way to evaluate them is to consider whether the diagnosis of MPD is real or whether it is manufactured by the therapist. It might be the case, for example, that a vulnerable patient is led to believe that he or she is in fact several different people/personalities and therefore the disorder of MPD develops as a consequence of the patient's interaction with the therapist, rather than arising spontaneously prior to therapy. In other words, is it iatrogenic or spontaneous? Iatrogenesis is an issue related to all illnesses — they may be manufactured or real.

Instead of being asked about case studies, you may be asked to discuss this issue of spontaneity versus iatrogenesis. Your answer should refer to psychological research (theory and/or studies), and can certainly be based around the case studies with which you are familiar.

You are required to produce a synoptic response, so some suggestions to help you with this task are included at the end of this topic (see p. 18). Questions will be designed to facilitate this.

What is multiple-personality disorder?

Multiple-personality disorder (MPD) is the existence within one person of two or more distinct personalities, each with unique and enduring characteristics. 'Alters' recurrently take control of the person's behaviour. Alters are often unaware of the other's thoughts and behaviour. The alternative name 'dissociative identity disorder' emphasises the fact that alters are dissociated, that is, have different consciousnesses. *DSM-IV* classifies MPD (DID) with other dissociative disorders (such as amnesia) and it is closely linked to post-traumatic stress disorder (PTSD) (see p. 32).

Case studies of MPD

Eve (Thigpen and Cleckley, 1954)

'Eve White', a 25-year-old married woman, was referred to a psychiatrist because she was having unexplained blackouts. During the course of therapy, another personality, 'Eve Black', emerged, who claimed that she had coexisted with Eve White since child-hood and was the cause of the blackouts when she 'came out'. Eve Black was quite different from the cautious, conservative and passive Eve White; she was flirtatious and lighthearted, and disdainful of Eve White's marriage and motherhood. Eve White was unaware of Eve Black but the reverse was not true. Personality tests showed significant differences between the two. Eve White was emotionally repressed and caring, whereas Eve Black was more childlike, intolerant and selfish — possibly they were the same person at different stages of development. The split may have occurred in childhood when Eve White felt deeply resentful of twin sisters and the personality dissociation was her way of coping. Later on, further personalities emerged: Jane, Evelyn and possibly another 20 more. In 1975, the real 'Eve' (Chris Sizemore) wrote her autobiography and claimed that she had learned to assimilate all her selves.

Jonah (Ludwig et al., 1972)

Jonah was hospitalised to investigate his bad headaches and memory lapses. Nurses noticed that his personality changed from time to time and, eventually, four distinct personalities were identified. They had all first emerged during Jonah's childhood, at times when he was under pressure. 'Sammy' provided help and sensible advice; he could coexist with Jonah or take over completely. 'King Young' was a ladies' man. 'Usoffa Abdulla' first emerged when Jonah was attacked by some boys and took the role of protector.

Sybil (Schreiber, 1973)

Sybil sought psychiatric treatment when she was a graduate student. It was during therapy that her alters emerged, as with Eve. In total, 17 alternative personalities emerged, including 'Mike', 'Sid' and a baby, 'Ruthie'. Subsequent analysis of the inter-views between Sybil and the psychiatrist, Cornelia Wilbur, suggested that the psychi-atrist had planted ideas in Sybil's mind and this is what led to the emergence of multiple personalities (Rieber, 1999).

Margaret (Dick-Barnes et al., 1987)

Margaret was the core personality of this 27-year-old female who had as many as 16 other personalities; three were usually present in any one day. Margaret was not very assertive and was left-handed. In contrast, one of her alters, Rachel, claimed to be 16 years old, was quite aggressive and sometimes worked as a prostitute. She was right-handed and appeared when there was a need to fight back. Dee was 8 years old and spoke like a child. She appeared to be the one who experienced the pain of emotional conflict; she held memories of sexual abuse and was ambidextrous.

Ken Bianchi, the 'Hillside Strangler' (Spanos et al., 1986)

When Ken Bianchi was accused of the brutal murders of 10 women in California, he claimed he had no knowledge of the murders but had experienced episodes of amnesia since childhood. During one interview, an alter called 'Steve' emerged and claimed responsibility for the killings. Experts interviewed him and decided that he was faking MPD. 'Steve' did not maintain a consistent personality, nor was there any independent evidence to support his claim of blackouts, unlike in Eve's case where her family gave evidence that supported Eve Black's stories.

Commentary on case studies

Case studies concern unique individuals. Such research provides rich details but makes generalisation difficult. The findings of these case studies are supported by larger-scale studies which demonstrate an increasing incidence of MPD. Such increases may be due to iatrogenesis or to the fact that therapists have become more accurate in diagnosing MPD.

One way to corroborate the evidence for separate personalities is to collect supporting evidence from relatives and friends (as in Eve's case). Another possibility is to produce physiological evidence of differences between personalities (e.g. using EEGs and galvanic skin responses). However, attempts to do this have not produced any reliable findings (Miller and Trigiano, 1992).

Is MPD spontaneous or iatrogenic?

Arguments for each position

Spontaneous

MPD occurs independently of therapist interaction. It is a coping mechanism which develops in certain individuals susceptible to dissociation and has been described as a highly creative survival technique.

Iatrogenic

MPD arises because therapists unknowingly elicit its symptoms by providing information about the disorder and they also teach the patient how to enact the roles of MPD. Certain individuals are suggestible, particularly if hypnotised, and they wish to please their therapist. These combined factors lead to MPD.

Case studies

Spontaneous

Eve's blackouts were confirmed by others over a long period of time. For example, Eve's husband once got very angry with her for buying some expensive clothes that she didn't recall buying.

Billy Milligan (Keyes, 1981) was acquitted of raping several women because he claimed that his lesbian personality 'Adelena' did it. The court regarded the condition as real.

Iatrogenic

Analysis of interviews with Sybil suggests that the therapist planted the idea in Sybil's mind. Sybil's desire to please the therapist may have led her to develop alternative personalities as suggested by the therapist.

Ken Bianchi manipulated the symptoms himself; but it has also been suggested that the evaluating psychiatrist may have elicited Bianchi's 'symptoms' by suggesting to Bianchi that there might be another part of him with whom he had not yet talked.

Over- and under-diagnosis
Spontaneous
Putnam et al. (1986) found that, on average, it took 7 years before MPD patients were diagnosed with the disease. This may be because the symptoms of MPD are similar to many other psychiatric diagnoses and MPD sufferers often also have secondary diagnoses of depression, anxiety or panic disorders.

MPD is more commonly diagnosed in women. However, it may be equally prevalent in men but they are more likely to be diagnosed with other mental illnesses, such as drug and alcohol abuse.

Iatrogenic
Modestin (1992) studied MPD rates in Switzerland and found that 50% of the cases were diagnosed by three psychiatrists. This may be because some psychiatrists encourage patients to develop MPD symptoms (iatrogenesis), or it may be that they recognise the disorder where others don't (spontaneous).

Empirical research evidence
Spontaneous
Scroppo et al. (1998) compared the symptoms of a set of MPD patients with other mentally ill patients. They concluded that the symptoms were quite different in each group. This supports the view that MPD sufferers have a distinct and real syndrome.

Iatrogenic
Spanos et al. (1985) hypnotised students and found that most of the students who were told that a part of themselves would feel differently did reveal a different person-ality, whereas if no suggestion was made they usually didn't. This suggests that at least certain people (those who are suggestible) respond to therapist suggestions.

Theoretical research evidence
Spontaneous
Dissociation is a real state as described by the neo-dissociation theory of hypnosis. Hilgard (1986) suggests that during hypnosis, consciousness is divided into several streams which are independent of each other. It is possible that people with MPD are able to self-hypnotise and dissociate parts of their consciousness from others.

Psychodynamic theory suggests that MPD is a way of coping with traumatic events such as sexual abuse. Conflict between the id, ego and superego results in the emergence of different personalities taking on different roles. In the case of Margaret, she was the superego, Rachel was the id and Dee was the ego.

Iatrogenic
MPD is a social construction. As people hear about the disorder, through the media and/or their therapist, its frequency increases. This may explain why MPD diagnoses

have increased. After Thigpen and Cleckley first published the case study of Eve, they were inundated by people claiming to have MPD, but only diagnosed one other true case (Thigpen and Cleckley, 1983).

Barber (1979) proposed an alternative explanation for hypnosis which would explain MPD too. Hypnosis occurs because individuals are acting out a social role — the role of being hypnotised — which is governed by social expectations about hypnotism. An MPD sufferer may be doing the same. This would explain why MPD is non-existent in some cultures (i.e. a culture-bound syndrome).

Synoptic overview

Different explanations or perspectives

Various explanations are offered to explain MPD: **psychodynamic**, **behaviourist** and **social constructionist**.

Demonstrating different methods used

Case studies are rich sources of data. Other methods have been used too, such as **experiments**, while some studies have recorded incidence rates (**observational studies**).

Relating overarching issues and debates

- **Gender bias** — MPD is more commonly diagnosed in women.
- **Cultural bias** — MPD may be a culture-bound syndrome; a social construction of our society.
- **Nature–nurture** — is MPD an inherited susceptibility or is it iatrogenic?
- **Forgetting** — context-dependent retrieval may explain why MPD sufferers exhibit behaviours in one situation rather than another. They have learned that some behaviours are appropriate in particular contexts.

Broad issues of psychological concern

- **Iatrogenesis** is an example of a demand characteristic and of participant reactivity.
- **Reliability** and **validity** are issues related to the diagnosis of MPD.

Culture-bound syndromes

Specification content

Case studies of syndromes apparently bound by culture (e.g. koro, dhat). Arguments for and against the existence of these culture-bound syndromes.

Case studies are again the focus of this topic area, in order to give you an understanding of culture-bound syndromes. Questions may be set asking you to describe and evaluate one or more case studies. This suggests that you need to know some case studies in considerable detail. You will not be asked about particular culture-bound syndromes. **Koro** and **dhat** are provided as examples of disorders that *may* be bound by culture.

The consideration of the case studies should lead you to form an opinion about whether culture-bound syndromes do or do not exist. You can use the case studies evidence, as well as other evidence, to support arguments for and/or against the existence of culture-bound syndromes.

If you are asked to present arguments *for* the existence of culture-bound syndromes, you should not assume that the arguments *against* will count as AO2. Counter-arguments are only credited as AO2 if they are used effectively as part of a critical assessment, not if they are just listed. So, if you list the arguments for and then list the arguments against, this would all be AO1 and only be creditworthy in a question that asked you to describe the arguments both for and against. Otherwise, you must set each counter-argument specifically against the argument it is countering.

You are required to produce a synoptic response, so some suggestions to help you with this task are included at the end of this topic (see p. 22). Questions will be designed to facilitate this.

Mental illness: absolute, universal or culturally relative

Absolute disorders occur in the same way and with the same frequency in all cultures. For example, chickenpox occurs all over the world with the same symptoms and similar rates of frequency. Schizophrenia may be absolute.

Universal disorders occur in all cultures but not with the same frequency. For example, coronary heart disease and depression occur more in industrial societies than in rural ones. The same may be true of some culture-bound syndromes. For example, **dhat** is a mental illness in which sufferers blame their physical and mental exhaustion on the presence of semen in their urine. Mumford (1996) concluded that dhat is more or less the same as depression but the symptoms differ among cultures. For example, more somatic symptoms occur in Indians — these might lead a Western doctor to diagnose a different illness.

Disorders that are **culturally relative** are unique (or almost unique) to particular cultures and only meaningful within those cultures. The term **culture-bound syndrome** (CBS) is used to refer to a disorder that is only recognised as an illness within a specific culture and where the symptoms do not fit any recognised Western category of mental disorder. In a true CBS, the culture-specific symptoms would be primary rather than being a cultural overlay of a universal mental disorder.

What are culture-bound syndromes?

CBSs are defined in *DSM-IV* as:

> ...recurrent, locality-specific patterns of aberrant behaviour and troubling experience that may or may not be linked to a particular *DSM-IV* diagnostic category. Many of these patterns are indigenously considered to be 'illnesses', or at least afflictions, and most have local names.

Case studies

Man goes amok in East Malaysia

A man aged 37 reportedly went berserk over his salary and smashed the windscreens of three vehicles, including a police patrol car. A six-man police team mounted an operation to track down the culprit and, when intercepted, the former timber camp worker dashed out from some bushes with a Samurai sword in his right hand and an iron hammer in the other. He was shot dead.   (*Daily Express*, February 2000)

Koro-like syndrome in a Jordanian male

A 24-year-old single, male, Jordanian farmer complained of a 2-week history of difficulty in getting to sleep, apprehension, isolation and fearfulness. The patient was convinced that his penis was gradually shrinking and would disappear into his abdomen. In great fear, he stated that he preferred death to such a fate. His one sexual experience was with a prostitute 1 month prior to the onset of his symptoms, after which he was left feeling guilty and embarrassed. He was diagnosed as having a generalised anxiety disorder and panic.   (Al-Hmoud, 1999)

A case study of neurasthenia

One patient was a 41-year-old man with headaches, pains in his joints, insomnia, loss of appetite, and the belief that there was something wrong with his brain that caused his scalp to sweat excessively. In treating him, the doctor diagnosed a skin disease of the scalp rather than a psychiatric disorder; the doctor claimed this would improve the scalp problem and through it the patient's depression. The doctor and patient perceived illness and treatment solely in somatic terms.   (Kleinman and Mechanic, 1981)

Case studies provide rich data about CBSs but are prone to researcher bias. The researchers and/or therapists offer their own interpretation of events which may be social constructions.

It is difficult to make objective judgements about what things mean to people from different cultures. For example, you may think that a set of symptoms describes depression, but those same symptoms may mean something quite different to a local person.

Arguments for and against the existence of culture-bound syndromes

At least seven broad categories can be differentiated among phenomena often described as CBSs (Hall, 1998). These are outlined below.

(1) An apparent mental illness recognised in certain cultures and which does not correspond to a recognised Western disease category
Example

Amok is found in Malaysia. An individual experiences a period of brooding followed by an outburst of violent, aggressive or homicidal behaviour directed at people and objects. The episode tends to be precipitated by a perceived insult or slight and seems to be prevalent only among males.

Evaluation

Schmidt et al. (1977) claim that all the cases they studied show signs of an underlying primary mental disorder, such as schizophrenia.

(2) An illness that may correspond to a subset of a Western disease category; it occurs in many cultural settings but is only elaborated as an illness in a few

Example

Koro (genital retraction syndrome) is found almost entirely in south and east Asia. It involves intense anxiety that the penis (or, in the rare female cases, the vulva and nipples) will recede into the body and possibly cause death. Occasionally the syndrome occurs in local epidemics.

Evaluation

Cases seem to be similar in many ways to the Western category of panic attack. Devan and Hong (1987) claim that there is a distinction between true koro and a 'koro-like state'. The latter occurs when an individual displays symptoms similar to koro but has a different underlying mental disorder (see the case study on page 20).

(3) A locally recognised mental illness which resembles a Western disease category but which lacks some of the symptoms of the Western disease

Example

Neurasthenia (shenjing shuairuo) is a Chinese version of major depressive disorder with more somatic than psychological symptoms, such as stomach pains.

Evaluation

The Chinese tend to somatose their symptoms (i.e. they complain of bodily pains rather than psychological problems such as sadness).

(4) A disease not yet recognised by Western medicine

Example

Kuru is a progressive psychosis and dementia found in cannibalistic tribes in New Guinea. The symptoms include palsy, contracted face muscles and loss of motor control.

Evaluation

It has been classified as a viral disease and is now believed to be a form of Creuzfeldt-Jakob disease.

(5) A culturally accepted explanation of an illness which would not make sense in a Western setting

Example

Witchcraft and religious/magical beliefs such as rootwork (Caribbean) or the evil eye (Mediterranean regions and Latin America).

Evaluation

Such 'explanations' may not be diagnoses of specific disorders.

(6) A state that locally is not seen as a mental illness but would be classified in this way in a Western setting

Example

Trance or possession states are regarded as 'normal' in some cultures but could indicate psychosis, delusions or hallucinations in a Western setting.

Evaluation

This may lead to different diagnoses in the West. Consider that black African–Caribbean immigrants in the UK are up to seven times more likely than white people to receive a diagnosis of schizophrenia (Cochrane and Sashidharan, 1995). This is possibly related to a misinterpretation of certain behaviours which are normal within that culture but viewed as abnormal in the West.

(7) A syndrome allegedly occurring in a given cultural setting and reported to the anthropologist or psychiatrist which does not in fact exist

Example

Windigo has been reported in the Algonkian Indians. This is a syndrome of cannibalistic obsessions whose reality has been challenged (Simons and Hughes, 1985).

Evaluation

Such explanations may, in fact, be used to justify the expulsion or execution of an outcast.

The concept of culture-bound syndromes

The concept of CBSs is useful because it brings culture to the attention of psychiatrists trained in a particular tradition. Awareness of CBSs allows psychiatrists and physicians to make more culturally appropriate diagnoses.

The concept is problematic, however, in that it is not a homogeneous category, and the designation of 'culture-bound' can imply that the illness is somehow 'not real', or that a patient's experience can be dismissed as merely 'exotic'.

Synoptic overview

Different explanations or perspectives

Culture-bound explanations can be contrasted with other perspectives on mental illness.

Demonstrating different methods used

Cross-cultural research has many limitations, such as observer bias.

Relating overarching issues and debates

Cultural bias — Western classification schemes are biased, leading to differential rates of diagnosis. The use of such schemes is an example of an imposed etic.

Links with other areas of the specification and other disciplines

AS individual differences — cultural relativism in the definitions of abnormality.
Psychopathology and **treatment of mental disorders** — cultural biases in these areas.

Psychopathology

Schizophrenia

Specification content

Clinical characteristics of schizophrenia. Biological (e.g. genetics, brain biochemistry) and psychological (e.g. social and family relationships) explanations of schizophrenia, including the evidence on which they are based.

You should be able to summarise some of the major clinical characteristics of schizophrenia. The most obvious way to do this is through a description of the symptoms of this mental disorder, although you could also respond appropriately by detailing the characteristics of different *types* of schizophrenia. The symptoms, and indeed the characteristics, of this disorder are extremely wide-ranging, so aim for some of the main ones, and don't worry about missing others.

You should be able to describe and evaluate at least *two* biological explanations of schizophrenia. Genetics and brain biochemistry (e.g. the dopamine hypothesis) are given as examples of appropriate biological explanations but there are others (such as brain dysfunction or viral infection). You should be able to describe and evaluate at least *two* psychological explanations too.

You may be asked to compare and contrast biological and psychological explanations, so make a note of similarities and differences in the two types of explanation. Don't miss the requirement for *evidence* in the specification entry. The most obvious way to provide evidence is by covering research studies that have explored the causes of schizophrenia.

You are required to produce a synoptic response, so some suggestions to help you with this task are included at the end of this topic (see p. 26). Questions will be designed to facilitate this.

Clinical characteristics of schizophrenia

DSM-IV describes several symptoms that a person must have before he or she is classified as having schizophrenia. These symptoms include two or more of the following behaviours for a duration of at least 1 month:

- **delusions** — bizarre beliefs that seem real to the person with schizophrenia but are not real. Sometimes these delusions can be paranoid in nature. Delusions may also involve beliefs relating to grandiosity.
- **hallucinations** — bizarre, unreal perceptions of the environment that may be auditory (hearing voices), visual (seeing lights, objects or faces), olfactory (smelling things) or tactile (e.g. feeling that bugs are crawling on or under the skin).
- **disorganised thinking/speech** — some people with schizophrenia speak very little; others have speech that is disjointed.

- **negative symptoms** — the absence of normal behaviour. Negative symptoms include social withdrawal, absence of emotion and expression, and reduced energy, motivation and activity.
- **catatonia** — immobility and 'waxy flexibility'. Catatonia is a negative symptom where people become fixed in a single position for a long period of time.

Biological explanations of schizophrenia

Biochemistry

Dopamine

The dopamine hypothesis states that schizophrenia is caused by an overactive dopamine system in the brain. Antipsychotic drugs block dopamine transmission and are therefore used to treat and improve the symptoms of schizophrenia.

Evidence for the dopamine hypothesis includes the findings that:
- drugs that block dopamine reduce schizophrenic symptoms
- drugs that block dopamine may have side effects similar to Parkinson's disease. Parkinson's disease is caused by a lack of dopamine in the basal ganglia in the brain.
- high doses of amphetamines (which increase dopamine activity) cause schizophrenic-like symptoms in a disorder known as 'amphetamine psychosis'. Drugs that block amphetamine psychosis also reduce schizophrenic symptoms, therefore strengthening the link between dopamine and schizophrenia.

Evidence against the dopamine hypothesis includes the findings that:
- amphetamines do more than just increase dopamine levels in the brain — they also alter levels of other neurotransmitters
- although antipsychotic drugs that block dopamine receptors act quickly, these drugs may take many days to change the behaviour of people with schizophrenia
- the effects of these drugs may be more indirect in that they may influence other systems that have more impact on actual schizophrenic symptoms

Serotonin

Drugs for schizophrenia that have been developed more recently block receptors for both dopamine and serotonin. Many patients for whom 'dopamine only' medication has not helped have benefited from medications that affect both dopamine and serotonin transmissions. This suggests that the neurotransmitter serotonin may also play a role in causing the symptoms of schizophrenia.

Genetics

Researchers have studied relatives of people with schizophrenia and have found that the illness runs in families. In other words, schizophrenia has an important genetic component. Evidence for a genetic component comes from twin and adoption studies.

Twin studies

Research has discovered that if one identical twin has schizophrenia, there is approximately a 50% chance that the other twin will develop the illness. The tendency for non-identical twins to develop schizophrenia is only about 15%. The figure for siblings (brothers or sisters) is also about 15%. Identical twins (monozygotic) have exactly the same genetic makeup, whereas non-identical (dizygotic or fraternal) twins share only half of their genetic makeup. If genetics were the only factor in developing schizophrenia, then both monozygotic twins should always develop the disorder. However, because the figure for monozygotic twins is much greater than that for dizygotic twins, this suggests that genetics *does* play a role, if not the whole role, in developing schizophrenia.

Adoption studies
Some studies have looked at people who were adopted at an early age and who later developed schizophrenia. One study (Kety et al., 1968) found that 13% of the biological relatives of adoptees who developed schizophrenia (yet had not interacted with the adoptee in any way) *also* had schizophrenia, whereas only 2% of the relatives of adoptees without schizophrenia had developed the disorder. Such studies also support the role of genetics in schizophrenia.

Psychological explanations of schizophrenia

Cognitive explanations
A common characteristic of individuals with schizophrenia is the inability to think clearly. Schizophrenia may have a relatively unique set of cognitive impairments of which working memory may be the core deficit. Prefrontal cortical regions in the brain are thought to play a crucial role in working memory. These deficits appear to be present before the onset of schizophrenia rather than being a consequence of the other symptoms associated with the illness.

Evidence for the role of cognitive functioning
Cognitive functioning may be markedly impaired in patients with schizophrenia but has only recently been recognised as an important factor in determining patient outcome. Cognitive impairment in schizophrenia, especially in working memory, is a strong predictor of outcome, whereas the degree to which an individual is affected by the positive symptoms of schizophrenia, such as hallucinations and delusions, is not a good predictor of outcome.

Research has shown that improvements in cognitive functioning occur independently of improvements in positive or negative clinical symptoms. Whereas typical antipsychotic drugs may improve clinical symptoms, they have little or no effect in improving cognitive dysfunction. Newer antipsychotic drugs, however, also appear to produce improvements in cognition (Keefe et al., 1999). Even though these newer medications improve cognition, they still do not normalise it, with many patients showing residual impairments in cognitive functioning.

Dysfunctional families
The theories of R. D. Laing in the 1960s appeared to 'blame' dysfunctional families for the development of schizophrenia in children and adolescents. In particular, the schizophrenic's mother was seen as the object of blame, being described as 'schizophrenogenic'. At that time, many psychiatrists held the view that the majority of cases

of schizophrenia were caused by mothers who were 'overanxious, obsessive, domineering and had a warped sex life'. Contradictory communication within the family (parents who express love and care, yet at the same time appear critical) led to the development of a 'double-bind' situation. This led to confusion and self-doubt, with the child eventually withdrawing from normal patterns of interaction. This view was largely abandoned during the 1970s, partly due to a lack of convincing evidence but mainly due to the advances being made in understanding the genetics and biochemistry of schizophrenia, thus making the practice of 'blaming the mother' unnecessary.

Expressed emotion

Expressed emotion (EE) is a family communication style that involves criticism, hostility and emotional over-involvement. High EE is related to the relapse of schizophrenia. Those living in families with high EE are nearly four times more likely to relapse than those living in families with low EE. In a study of the relapse rates among schizophrenics in Iran, Kalafi and Torabi (1996) found that the high prevalence of EE in Iranian culture (overprotective mothers and rejective fathers) was one of the main causes of schizophrenic relapses. In a meta-analysis of 27 studies of EE and schizophrenia outcomes, Butzlaff and Hooley (1998) confirmed that EE is a significant predictor of relapse in schizophrenia. In particular, they found that the EE–relapse relationship was strongest for patients with more chronic schizophrenic illness.

Synoptic overview

Different explanations or perspectives

Biological (biochemistry and genetics) and **psychological** (cognitive, dysfunctional families, expressed emotion) explanations have been proposed.

Demonstrating different methods used

Twin and **adoption studies** have been used to demonstrate the heritability of schizophrenia.

Meta-analyses have shown the importance of high expressed emotion for relapse rates.

Relating overarching issues and debates

Nature–nurture — twin and adoption studies have demonstrated the importance of a genetic predisposition for schizophrenia.

Determinism — although twin studies have provided evidence for a genetic predisposition to schizophrenia, none has shown 100% concordance in MZ twins.

Role of cultural factors — schizophrenia has been linked with cultures where high expressed emotion in families is the norm.

Historical bias — the idea of dysfunctional families causing schizophrenia was largely abandoned during the 1970s because of the advances in the genetics and biochemistry of schizophrenia, thus making 'blaming the mother' unnecessary.

Links with other areas of the specification and other disciplines

Other disciplines — the study and treatment of Parkinson's disease has highlighted the importance of dopamine for Parkinson's and schizophrenia.

Depression

Specification content

Clinical characteristics of depression (e.g. bipolar disorder, unipolar disorder). Biological (e.g. genetics, biochemistry) and psychological (e.g. learned helplessness) explanations of depression, including the evidence on which they are based.

You should be able to summarise some of the major clinical characteristics of depression. As with schizophrenia, the most obvious way to do this is through a description of the *symptoms*, although you could also respond appropriately by detailing the characteristics of different *types* of depression (unipolar, bipolar etc.). You should be able to describe and evaluate at least two biological explanations of depression. Genetics and brain biochemistry (e.g. neurotransmitter explanations) are given as examples of appropriate biological explanations but there are others (e.g. the role of melatonin in seasonal affective disorder). Likewise, you should be able to describe and evaluate at least two psychological explanations as well. You may be asked to compare and contrast biological and psychological explanations of depression, so make a note of similarities and differences as part of your revision.

You are required to produce a synoptic response, so some suggestions to help you with this task are included at the end of this topic (see p. 31). Questions will be designed to facilitate this.

Clinical characteristics of depression

Within the *DSM-IV* classification of mental disorders, there are two categories of depression: major depression (or unipolar disorder) and bipolar disorder. Major depression is by far the more common form of the disorder. The formal diagnosis of major depression requires the presence of five of the following symptoms (including either depressed mood or loss of interest and pleasure):

- sad, depressed mood
- loss of interest and pleasure in usual activities
- difficulties in sleeping (insomnia) or in some patients a desire to sleep all the time
- a shift in activity level, becoming either lethargic or agitated
- poor appetite and weight loss, or increased appetite and weight gain
- loss of energy and great fatigue
- negative self-concept, feelings of worthlessness and guilt
- difficulty in concentrating, such as slowed thinking and indecisiveness
- recurrent thoughts of death or suicide

What causes depression?

- Biochemistry — deficiencies in serotonin and norepinephrine are thought to be responsible for certain symptoms of depression, including anxiety, irritability and fatigue.

- Genetics — depression can run in families. For example, if one identical twin has depression, the other twin has a 70% chance of having the illness at some time in his/her life.
- Personality — people with low self-esteem, who are easily overwhelmed by stress or who are generally pessimistic, appear to be vulnerable to depression.
- Environmental factors — continuous exposure to violence, neglect, abuse or poverty may make people who are already susceptible to depression more vulnerable to the illness.

Biological explanations of depression

Neurotransmitter theories

Norepinephrine (noradrenaline)

In the 1960s, it was proposed that depression stems from a deficiency of norepinephrine in certain brain circuits. The theory has since been refined, acknowledging, for instance, that decreases or elevations in norepinephrine do not alter mood in everyone.

Among the findings linking impoverished synaptic norepinephrine levels to depression is the discovery in many studies that indirect markers of norepinephrine levels in the brain (levels of its by-products in more accessible material, such as urine) are often low in depressed individuals. In addition, post-mortem studies have revealed increased densities of certain norepinephrine receptors in the cortex of depressed suicide victims.

It might appear that elevated numbers of receptors would mean more contact between norepinephrine and its receptors and therefore more signal transmission. But when transmitter molecules become unusually scarce in synapses, postsynaptic cells often expand receptor numbers in a compensatory attempt to pick up whatever signals are available.

Serotonin

Early explanations held that depletion of serotonin at synapses was another cause of depression — one that worked by promoting, or 'permitting', a fall in norepinephrine levels. Serotonin depletion might contribute to depression by affecting other kinds of neurone too; serotonin-producing cells extend into many brain regions thought to participate in depressive symptoms.

Among the findings supporting a link between low synaptic serotonin levels and depression is that cerebrospinal fluid in depressed, and especially suicidal, patients contains reduced amounts of a major serotonin by-product (signifying reduced levels of serotonin in the brain itself).

Further evidence comes from the therapeutic effectiveness of drugs that block presynaptic reuptake transporters from drawing serotonin out of the synaptic cleft. Tricyclic antidepressants produce many effects in the brain, including a decrease in serotonin reuptake and a consequent rise in serotonin levels at synapses. The introduction of Prozac and other drugs able to block serotonin reuptake transporters without affecting other brain monoamines has confirmed this association between serotonin and depression.

Commentary on the role of neurotransmitters in depression

Norepinephrine and serotonin are clearly the main neurotransmitters implicated in depression, yet their exact contribution is still open to question. Comer (1995) suggests several possibilities:

- *Low norepinephrine and low serotonin combine to cause depression*. This argument suggests that depression will only be experienced when levels of both neurotransmitters are low and will lift only when levels of both neurotransmitters are raised. However, the fact that significant improvement can be achieved when the levels of only one neurotransmitter are raised casts doubts on this argument.
- *Low levels of either neurotransmitter can lead to depression*. Research studies have shown that some depressed people have low levels of norepinephrine by-products in their urine (reflecting low levels of norepinephrine in the brain), while others have low levels of serotonin by-products (reflecting low levels of serotonin in the brain). Similarly, when tryptophan (a precursor of serotonin) is administered, it alleviates depressive symptoms in some people. When tyrosine (a precursor of norepinephrine) is administered, it alleviates depressive symptoms in others.
- *Norepinephrine depression is different from serotonin depression*. Depressed subjects with low serotonin levels tend to be more apathetic and suicidal than depressed subjects with more normal serotonin levels (Asberg et al., 1976).
- *Neither norepinephrine nor serotonin supplies are key factors in depression*. Some researchers believe that the problem lies not with norepinephrine or serotonin levels, but with ineffective norepinephrine or serotonin receptors that fail to capture sufficient of these neurotransmitters, thus creating the impression that they are depleted in the brain. There is also some evidence that high levels of acetylcholine may cause depression. Exposure to certain potent insecticides causes an increase in acetylcholine levels and such patients may undergo a depressive change in mood.

Genetics and depression

Based on data that major depression clusters in families, having a first-degree relative (parent or sibling) with depression is a risk factor. Although results from family or twin studies have not been definitive in showing the exact contribution of genetics to depression, evidence is accumulating that there is a genetic risk and that this may be different for women and men (APA, 2002).

Between 1992 and 1993, each member of 2685 twin pairs was interviewed over the telephone. Looking at whether depression had occurred in both or only one twin of a pair enabled the researchers to estimate the heritability of the disorder. For the women in the sample, heritability ranged from 36% to 44%. For the men, the range was from 1% to 24%. The researchers concluded that individual environmental factors appear to play a greater role in the development of male depression (Bierut et al., 1999).

Sex hormones

The link between increased rates of depression and puberty, mood and the menstrual cycle, as well as mood and pregnancy, suggests a role of gonadal hormones in depression. Specifically, changes in gonadal hormones, disturbances in the hypothalamic–pituitary–gonadal (HPG) axis and attendant effects on neuromodulators (e.g. serotonin) may all be key mechanisms in the initiation of depression. For example, pregnancy and birth produce dramatic changes in oestrogen and progesterone levels, as well as changes in the HPG axis, which may underlie postpartum depression (APA, 2002).

Psychological explanations of depression

Life stress and trauma

Studies have shown that more than 80% of major depression cases are preceded by a serious adverse life event (e.g. bereavement or divorce). Traumatic events, such as childhood sexual abuse, adult sexual assault, male partner violence and physical illness, can also lead to depression. Initial research has suggested that early trauma has a greater impact on risk for depression than later-occurring trauma. Research has also indicated that women may be more likely than men to experience depression in response to a stressful event (APA, 2002).

Learned helplessness (Seligman, 1974)

Depression may be learned when people try but fail to control unpleasant experiences; whatever they do is futile. As a result, they acquire a sense of being unable to exercise control over their life, and so become depressed. This 'learned helplessness' then impairs their performance in situations that can be controlled, a characteristic of many depressives who fail to initiate coping strategies in the face of stress. The 'reformulated helplessness theory' (Abramson et al., 1978) stresses the importance of how depressed people think about failure. Typically, they believe that the source of such events is internal ('It's my fault, I'm stupid'), stable ('People will never want to be my friend') and global ('Everything I do goes wrong'). People who are prone to depression are thus thought to show a depressive attributional style, where they attribute bad outcomes to personal, stable and global character faults.

Learned helplessness has been demonstrated in many human studies. Hiroto and Seligman (1974) showed that college students who were exposed to uncontrollable aversive events were more likely to fail on cognitive tasks. Wu et al. (1999) found that uncontrollable negative events (associated with a learned helplessness task) led to lower levels of serotonin, providing a link with biological explanations of depression.

Gender differences in depression

More women than men are diagnosed with depression. Although there is no one explanation for this, there are several possibilities (Comer, 1995).

- *The artefact hypothesis*. This suggests that men and women are equally prone to depression but because men may find it less socially acceptable to seek treatment, their depression is less easily diagnosed. Men may use alcohol abuse as a way of dealing with their depression; the ratio of male to female alcoholics is the same as the ratio of female to male depressives.

- *Psychoanalytic explanations*. During the Oedipal stage of development, the girl realises she lacks a penis and believes herself to have been castrated by her mother. She feels both hostility and a sense of inferiority. As a result, women become more vulnerable to loss and thus more prone to depression.
- *Sociocultural explanations*. The role that many women play in society makes them vulnerable to depression. As the housewife role provides them with limited sources of gratification, they may become depressed. Alternatively, working women may become depressed because they bear the double burden of housework and a job outside the home.
- *The learned helplessness explanation*. Women are more vulnerable to depression because they are more likely to feel that they have no control over their lives. Laboratory tests have shown that women are more prone to learned helplessness effects than men.

Synoptic overview

Different explanations and perspectives
Biological (neurotransmitters, genetics, sex hormones) and **psychological** (life stress and trauma, interpersonal relationships and cognitive styles) explanations.

Demonstrating different methods used
Twin studies — Bierut et al. (1999).
Clinical output studies — evidence for the role of serotonin in depression comes from the therapeutic effectiveness of SSRIs such as Prozac.
Case studies — these have shown that more than 80% of major depression cases are preceded by a serious adverse life event (e.g. bereavement or divorce).

Relating overarching issues and debates
Nature–nurture — twin studies suggest that there is a genetic predisposition to depression.
Gender issues — gender differences in depression are explained by the artefact hypothesis, learned helplessness and sociocultural explanations.

Links with other areas of the specification and other disciplines
Psychoanalysis — during the Oedipal stage of development, the girl believes herself to have been castrated by her mother. As a result, women become more vulnerable to loss and thus more prone to depression.

Anxiety disorders

Specification content

Clinical characteristics of any one anxiety disorder (e.g. post-traumatic stress disorder, phobic disorders, obsessive–compulsive disorder). Biological (e.g. genetics, biochemistry) and psychological (e.g. conditioning) explanations of the chosen disorder, including the evidence on which they are based.

It is best to break this section of the specification into its constituent parts. This is an important exercise, as question setters look to all the aspects as potential parts of a question. Don't expect every question to be 'Discuss explanations of *one* type of anxiety disorder'.

You may be asked to outline the clinical characteristics of one of the anxiety disorders listed above — the simplest way to do this is in terms of the symptoms of your chosen disorder. For the sake of brevity, only post-traumatic stress disorder and phobic disorders are covered here and you only need to study one of these.

You need to know two different types of biological explanation for your chosen disorder — it is important to include at least two types because, if you are asked for 'types' in the plural, you will lose marks if you give only one. This diversity will also contribute to the 'synoptic' requirement (and so will earn you higher marks if done well). In the same way, you need to know two different types of psychological explanation for your chosen disorder.

Finally, you must study research evidence supporting (or challenging) these explanations — this might be requested as AO1 (in which case a description of research evidence will be required) or may be used as part of your AO2 content. If you use research evidence as AO2, don't forget to preface it with lead-in phrases such as 'This explanation is supported by…'.

The clinical characteristics are only ever AO1. (It would be difficult to imagine what one might write as AO2 for these!) However, the different explanations do need to be evaluated, so choose ones to which you can contribute some AO2 discussion.

You are required to produce a synoptic response, so some suggestions to help you with this task are included at the end of this topic (see p. 36). Questions will be designed to facilitate this.

Clinical characteristics of anxiety disorders

Post-traumatic stress disorder (PTSD)

PTSD arises as a delayed and/or protracted response to a stressful event or situation (either short- or long-lasting) of an exceptionally threatening or catastrophic nature, which is likely to cause pervasive distress in almost anyone. Such events include natural or man-made disasters, combat, serious accidents, witnessing the violent death of others, or being the victim of torture, terrorism, rape or other crime. Typical symptoms include:

- episodes of repeated reliving of the trauma in intrusive memories ('flashbacks') or dreams, occurring against the persisting background of a sense of emotional 'numbness'
- detachment from other people, unresponsiveness to surroundings and avoidance of activities and situations reminiscent of the trauma
- fear and avoidance of cues that remind the sufferer of the original trauma
- a state of autonomic hyperarousal, an enhanced startle reaction and insomnia

Anxiety and depression are commonly associated with the above symptoms and signs, and thoughts of suicide are not infrequent.

Phobic disorders

Agoraphobia is a term used to indicate fears not only of open spaces but also of related aspects, such as the presence of crowds and the difficulty of immediate easy escape to a safe place (usually home). The term therefore refers to an often overlapping cluster of phobias embracing fears of leaving home, crowds, entering shops, public places or travelling alone in trains, buses or planes.

Although the severity of the anxiety and the extent of avoidance behaviour are variable, many sufferers are terrified by the thought of collapsing and being left helpless in public. The lack of an immediately available exit is one of the key features of many of these agoraphobic situations. Most sufferers are women and the onset is usually early in adult life.

Social phobias often start in adolescence and are centred upon a fear of scrutiny by other people in comparatively small groups (as opposed to crowds), leading to an avoidance of social situations. They may be discrete (e.g. restricted to eating in public, public speaking or encounters with the opposite sex) or diffuse, involving almost all social situations outside the family circle. Characteristics of social phobias include:
- complaints of flushing, hand tremor, nausea, or the urgent need to urinate
- fear of vomiting in public, which may progress to panic attacks
- low self-esteem and fear of criticism
- avoidance of social situations and, in extreme cases, almost complete social isolation

Specific phobias are restricted to distinct situations. Fears include proximity to particular animals, heights, thunder, darkness, flying, closed spaces, eating certain foods, the sight of blood or injury, and exposure to specific diseases. Although the triggering situation is discrete, contact with it can evoke panic, as in social phobias. Specific phobias usually arise in childhood or early adult life and can persist for decades if they remain untreated. The seriousness of the resulting handicap depends on how easy it is for the sufferer to avoid the phobic situation. Fear of the phobic situation tends not to fluctuate, in contrast to agoraphobia.

Psychological explanations of phobic disorders

Sociocultural factors

Threatening environments

Phobic disorders are more likely to develop in people who are confronted with societal pressures and situations that pose real danger. Studies (e.g. Baum and Fleming, 1993) have shown that people in highly threatening environments are more likely to develop the general feelings of tension, anxiety and fatigue that characterise generalised anxiety disorders and the specific fears and avoidance behaviours that characterise phobic disorders. In the months after the Three Mile Island nuclear reactor accident, mothers of preschool children who lived in the vicinity were found to display five times as many anxiety disorders as mothers of comparable age and family structure living elsewhere (Baum, 1990). The Three Mile Island mothers still displayed elevated levels of anxiety a year after the accident.

Poverty

One of the most direct indicators of societal stress is poverty. People without sufficient means typically live in homes that are more run down and communities with higher crime rates; they have fewer educational and job opportunities and are at greater risk of health problems. Research indicates that poorer people have higher rates of phobic and generalised anxiety disorders. For example, research has shown that those who rely primarily on welfare or disability benefits for their income show a much greater prevalence of phobias than other people (Eaton et al., 1991). Although poverty and other societal pressures may establish a climate in which phobic and generalised anxiety disorders are more likely to develop, sociocultural variables are not the only factors at work. After all, most people in war-torn, politically oppressed or endangered communities do not develop anxiety disorders. Theorists must still explain why some people develop these disorders and others do not.

Learning — classical and operant conditioning

Mowrer's two-factor conditioning theory suggests that:

- the intensity of the traumatic incident is such that stimuli that were present at the time of the trauma (unconditioned stimulus) become associated with fear and arousal symptoms
- similar (conditioned) stimuli trigger responses as if the trauma was recurring
- through stimulus generalisation, a wide variety of stimuli bearing any slight resemblance to the actual traumatic stimuli become triggers for the distress associated with the original stimulus
- the person tries to avoid all the distressing stimuli in their environment. Although it provides less distress, it is this avoidance behaviour that maintains and reinforces the deep-seated fear, preventing extinction and thus maintaining the problem which is clinically labelled as post-traumatic stress disorder

Psychological explanations of PTSD

Early experiences

For some people, anxiety may persist well after a traumatic situation is over. Unlike other anxiety disorders, which are typically triggered by objects or situations that most people would not find threatening, situations that cause PTSD would be traumatic for anyone. Recent studies have shown that childhood events seem to leave some people vulnerable to developing PTSDs in response to later traumatic experiences. People whose childhoods have been characterised by poverty, whose family members suffered mental disorders, or who experienced assault or abuse at an early age, are more likely to develop PTSD in the face of later trauma than are people without such childhood experiences (Kolb, 1992).

It has been suggested that the tendency of many abused children to dissociate themselves from the experience and memory of abuse may become a habitual way of dealing with traumatic events in life. This leads them to 'blot out' later traumas too, setting the stage for the development of PTSD (Bremner, 1993). Other studies suggest that people with certain personality profiles are more likely to develop these disorders. It has been found, for example, that rape victims who had psychological problems before they were assaulted and war veterans who had poor relationships before they went into combat run a risk of developing prolonged stress reactions after traumatic experiences.

Personality

The idea that personality is related in some way to vulnerability to PTSD is further supported by research by Kobasa (1990) who discovered that many people respond to stress with a set of positive attitudes that she collectively referred to as **hardiness**. These help people to carry on their lives with a sense of fortitude, control and commitment. Those who showed fewer traits of hardiness showed less ability to deal with traumatic events in such a constructive way. It has also been shown that people who are helped by strong social support systems (e.g. family and friends) after a traumatic event are less likely to develop an extended disorder such as PTSD. Research has shown, too, that weak social support networks have contributed to the development of PTSD in, for example, Vietnam war veterans (Figley and Leventman, 1990).

Extreme trauma

Although childhood experiences, personality and social support play important roles in a person's reactions to stress, the events that trigger PTSD can sometimes be so extreme and traumatic that they override a positive childhood, hardy personality and supportive social context. In a follow-up study of 253 Vietnam prisoners of war, it was discovered that 5 years after their release, 23% still required psychiatric help, despite the fact that all had been evaluated as well adjusted before their imprisonment. It was found that those who had been imprisoned the longest and treated the most harshly showed the highest percentage of anxiety-related disorders (Ursano et al., 1981). Likewise, those who had witnessed the worst atrocities later experienced the most severe symptoms of PTSD (Yehuda et al., 1992).

Biological explanations of PTSD

A number of biological factors have been linked to PTSD symptoms. It has been claimed that they make people with PTSD hyper-responsive to stressful stimuli, especially those that are reminiscent of the trauma (Ray, 2002).

The hippocampus

Stress causes the adrenal glands to release cortisol. Excessive amounts of hormones such as cortisol damage the hippocampus, a memory centre in the brain. Using MRI scans, Bremner (1997) found smaller hippocampi in PTSD patients, compared with the hippocampi of matched control subjects. Disturbances of hippocampal function may lead to enhanced reactivity to stimulation and the cognitive deficits found in PTSD patients.

Neuroendocrinological abnormalities

Vietnam war veterans with PTSD have been found to have higher levels of corticotrophin-releasing factor, which may be the reason behind their high anxiety and fear-related behaviours. High levels of adrenaline and noradrenaline in patients with PTSD are consistent with a chronic stress reaction. In keeping with the enhanced secretion of these stress hormones, patients with PTSD show an enhanced startle response and higher heart rates and blood pressure. In a study of PTSD (Southwick et al., 1993), stimulating the noradrenergic part of the nervous system caused flash-backs and panic attacks in PTSD patients but not in controls.

Genetics

In one study of Vietnam war veterans (Reich et al., 1996), which compared the family histories of probands with PTSD and probands with other anxiety disorders, a much greater incidence of PTSD was found in the family histories of PTSD probands than in any of the other groups.

Synoptic overview

Different explanations or perspectives

Anxiety disorders can be explained from different **biological** and **psychological** perspectives.

Demonstrating different methods used

A variety of different investigative methods have been used to study the development of anxiety disorders, including family history studies, twin studies, adoption studies, psychometric tests and experiments.

MRI scans — the use of magnetic resonance imaging has found that people with PTSD have decreased hippocampal volume.

Relating overarching issues and debates

Nature–nurture — family and twin studies suggest that there is a genetic pre-disposition to phobic anxiety disorders and PTSD.

Links with other areas of the specification and other disciplines

AS physiological psychology — prolonged exposure to stress (PTSD) may lead to the depletion of the neurotransmitter noradrenaline.

Treating mental disorders

Biological (somatic) therapies

Specification content

Use and mode of action of chemotherapy, ECT and psychosurgery. Issues surrounding the use of such therapies (e.g. appropriateness and effectiveness).

In this area of the specification, the same requirement is made for all therapies studied: you should know about how they are used and how they work (their mode of action). You should also study issues that surround the use of the therapy. Such issues are likely to concern appropriateness and effectiveness but might also, for example, include ethical issues or questions about reliability and validity.

Three forms of biological (somatic) therapy are named in the specification — chemotherapy, ECT and psychosurgery — which means that you may be set questions specifically on any or all of these therapies. For each of them you must be able to suggest when such a therapy is used (for example, ECT is used mainly for depression) and how the therapy works (for example, ECT works by administering a weak electrical current to the brain, usually over six treatment sessions). Such knowledge and understanding would form the AO1 part of any answer.

In addition, you should be able to evaluate these methods. This might be achieved through a consideration of their appropriateness. For example, is it appropriate to use ECT bearing in mind potential ethical objections? Evaluation might also be achieved through a consideration of effectiveness. This might be established with reference to research studies that do or do not show effectiveness. It is possible to evaluate any research study in terms of relevant methodological issues, too. Further evaluation can be achieved by comparing any of the biological therapies with each other and/or with alternative therapies. However, AO2 marks would only be awarded where other therapies are used as part of a sustained critical argument. There are no marks available for a description of other therapies.

You might be asked a question solely on the issues surrounding the use of biological therapies, in which case a description of their use and mode of action may be largely irrelevant. If you are asked to 'compare and contrast' biological therapies with another group of therapies, then you will gain marks for *describing* them, but none for any evaluation. AO2 marks in 'compare and contrast' questions are given for consideration of similarities and differences. It is imperative that you focus on the demands of any particular question and do not waste time including uncreditworthy material.

You are required to produce a synoptic response, so some suggestions to help you with this task are included at the end of this topic (see p. 41). Questions will be designed to facilitate this.

Chemotherapy

Main class of drug	Use	Mode of action
Antianxiety drugs (e.g. benzodiazepines such as Valium)	To reduce anxiety	Enhance GABA activity — a natural form of anxiety relief which slows down nerve cell activity and reduces serotonin activity; serotonin is a neurotransmitter which stimulates some neurones
Antipsychotic drugs, either the older 'typical' drugs such as haloperidol or the newer 'atypical' drugs such as risperidone	To treat psychotic disorders such as schizophrenia	Block dopamine receptor sites; dopamine is a neuro-transmitter associated with schizophrenia
Antidepressant drugs (e.g. serotonin reuptake inhibitors, SSRIs, such as Prozac)	To treat unipolar depression	Block reuptake of serotonin at synapses and thus promotes serotonin activity
Antimanic drugs (e.g. lithium carbonate)	To treat bipolar depression	Enhance uptake of serotonin and norepinephrine, thereby reducing the action of both these neurotransmitters
Stimulants (e.g. ritalin)	To treat ADD (attention-deficit disorder)	Stimulate the central nervous system, increasing attention span and ability to focus while decreasing restlessness

Issues surrounding use

Appropriateness

Strengths

- Drug therapies use knowledge about physiological mechanisms. For example, depression has been linked to low levels of serotonin as a cause. Therefore enhancing serotonin levels makes sense as a treatment.
- Many patients (and doctors) prefer drug therapies to psychological approaches because they require little effort and provide a quick response.
- Drugs may also be used with psychological methods to provide a window of opportunity within which alternative appropriate courses of treatment may be started.

Limitations

- Side effects: headaches, nausea, vomiting, dry mouth, motor restlessness, sleep disturbances.
- Addiction: benzodiazepines are addictive and should only be taken for short periods. Other drugs may be psycho-addictive.
- Drugs treat the symptoms, not the causes.

Effectiveness

- Placebo-controlled trials are used to distinguish between the pharmacological and psychological effects of drugs.

- The newer 'atypical' drugs used to treat schizophrenia produce fewer side effects but are no more effective than the older drugs (Geddes et al. 2000, a survey of over 50 clinical trials).
- The *NHSdirect* website cites 50–60% success rates for antidepressant drugs.
- However, Moore (1999) reports that in FDA trials nearly 90% of the improvements reported by patients taking Prozac were also reported by the patients taking placebos, suggesting that drug effectiveness may be just as much psychological as pharmacological.

ECT (electroconvulsive therapy)

Use

ECT is used as a treatment for depression and, occasionally, for other mental illnesses, including mania and schizophrenia. It has been used since the 1930s, but has been greatly refined in recent years and is now much safer and more acceptable. It is not necessarily always used as a last resort but it is used when depression is severe or when other treatments have produced negative results in the past for individual patients. In addition, some patients cannot tolerate antidepressants (although this is less common with new drugs).

Mode of action

The patient is given a muscle relaxant and general anaesthetic. A low voltage electric shock (70–130 volts) is applied for about 2 seconds, usually bilaterally (i.e. to both sides of the brain). This leads to an artificial epileptic fit, which is reduced by the muscle relaxant so that the body hardly moves. The patient wakes up within 5 minutes and goes to the recovery room. Patients are only aware of having gone to sleep.

Treatments are generally given twice or three times weekly. A total of between six and twelve treatments is usual but some patients need more for full recovery. After a course of ECT, treatment for depression needs to continue to maintain recovery. This is often an antidepressant but can take the form of further ECT.

Why does it work? It may be that ECT restores the abnormal neurotransmitter levels in depressed individuals (see neurotransmitter explanations of depression on pages 28–29). Alternatively, it may be that the memory loss associated with ECT allows restructuring of disordered thinking.

Issues surrounding use

Appropriateness

Strengths
- ECT works more quickly and more effectively than antidepressants in the short-term treatment of severe depression.

Limitations
- Side effects include headache, nausea and muscle aches during the morning of the treatment. Some people suffer from memory problems.
- There is a slight risk from the use of anaesthetic, but no evidence of any brain damage caused by the electrical current.

Effectiveness

Sackeim et al. (2001) studied nearly 300 patients who completed an ECT course; 60% responded to treatment. However, there appeared to be quite a high relapse rate within a year (about 60%), suggesting that relief was temporary and not a cure (Sackeim et al., 1993). It is recommended that ECT should always be followed up with maintenance treatment.

Certain patients appear to be more likely to benefit, for example those who relapse frequently despite taking antidepressants and those who have more biological symptoms (i.e. are not depressed because of life problems but whose depression is more related to biochemical changes in the body).

Psychosurgery

Use

Psychosurgery is usually used to treat severe, incapacitating, non-schizophrenic mood disorders when all other attempts at treatment have failed and the alternative is continued suffering for the patient.

Mode of action

Early methods (1930s–1950s) involved the removal of the large portions of the frontal cortex (the part behind the forehead), or cutting the fibres running from the frontal lobes to other parts of the brain. **Prefrontal lobotomy** was performed to induce personality changes and make a patient more controllable.

Recent psychosurgery only involves functional deconnection of parts of the frontal lobes of the brain, specifically the parts concerned with emotional response (the limbic system). 'Functional deconnection' means that these parts are not removed but the connections are destroyed so that it is as if they have been removed. **Stereotactic neurosurgical techniques** (e.g. stereotactic subcaudate tractotomy, SST) involve the use of specially constructed frames which are attached to the patient's skull, together with neuro-imaging (CT or MRI scans). This allows precise guidance (to within 1 millimetre) of special probes to any desired target within the brain.

The procedure is carried out under general anaesthetic and lasts about 90 minutes, most of this time being taken up with X-rays to monitor the position of the probe. A lesion is produced using radio-frequency (heat) or electric current.

Issues surrounding use
Appropriateness
Strengths
- Psychosurgery is effective as a treatment of last resort.

Limitations
- The patient undergoes an irreversible operation with possible side effects such as: confusion, which lasts up to a month and sometimes longer; fits and cerebral haemorrhage; apathy; excessive weight gain; and disinhibition.
- Rehabilitation must be gradual, because recovery is a slow process.

Effectiveness

Bartlett et al. (1994) reported that SST allowed 40–60% of patients to live normal or near-normal lives. In the UK, of 42 patients on whom data were available, significant improvement was reported by doctors in 12, some improvement in 22, no change in six, some deterioration in two and significant deterioration in none.

Cosgrove et al. (1996) reported successful treatment of patients with depressive or anxiety disorders using **cingulotomies** (functional deconnection of the cingulated gyrus). These patients had not benefited from any other available therapies.

Synoptic overview

Different explanations or perspectives

Compare and contrast this therapeutic approach with other approaches in psychology, provided that such comparison is used effectively.

Relating overarching issues and debates

- **Cultural bias** — each of these therapies is related to a particular historical period. Drug therapy is currently very popular.
- **Ethical issues** — individual rights must be balanced against the protection of other people.

This approach to treatment is both **reductionist** and **determinist**. It also de-emphasises the role of **nurture** in mental illness.

Links with other areas of the specification and other disciplines

- **AS physiological psychology** — antianxiety drugs are used to treat stress; can be contrasted with other stress management methods.
- **AS individual differences** — assumptions of the biological model in terms of its view on treatment.
- **Other treatments** — compare and contrast with other therapeutic measures.

Behavioural therapies

Specification content

Use and mode of action of behavioural therapies, including those based on classical (e.g. flooding) and operant (e.g. token economies) conditioning. Issues surrounding the use of such therapies (e.g. appropriateness and effectiveness).

The same principles apply here as for the biological therapies — you need to cover their use, mode of action and issues surrounding their application.

Note that here, as before, you are required to study more than one therapy. In the case of behavioural therapies it is specified that you study at least *one* therapy that is based on classical conditioning, such as flooding, and *one* therapy based on operant conditioning, such as token economies. This means that you can be asked questions about therapies based on classical and/or operant conditioning (because these are named in the specification) but not be asked questions specifically on flooding or token economies (because these are given as examples only).

You should be aware of the AO1 and AO2 material that may be required in an exam question. You may be asked to describe (AO1) and evaluate (AO2) the behavioural therapies. You may be asked to describe and evaluate issues surrounding the use of behavioural therapies. In both cases, it would be sufficient to focus on two therapies but better to demonstrate a slightly wider knowledge. However, you must consider the balance between depth and breadth. If you try to cover too many therapies (breadth) you inevitably have less time in an exam to record details (depth), which results in a loss of AO1 marks (one of the criteria for AO1 marks is the amount of detail provided, but stronger answers achieve a balance between depth and breadth).

Finally, you may be asked to compare and contrast behavioural therapies with, for example, biological therapies. It may be a good idea to consider the similarities and differences between these two categories when you are revising. This will be helpful if you have to answer such a question and will also increase your understanding of the two different kinds of therapy. If you are asked, for example, to compare and contrast behavioural therapies with biological therapies, then the AO1 content can be a description of both kinds of therapy and the AO2 content can be a consideration (description and/or evaluation) of the similarities and differences between them. Alternatively, AO1 is a description of similarities and AO2 is an evaluation of these.

You are required to produce a synoptic response, so some suggestions to help you with this task are included at the end of this topic (see p. 47). Questions will be designed to facilitate this.

Behavioural therapies: general issues

The behavioural approach is concerned only with what you can see, and therefore treatments deal with observable behaviour only. There is no attempt to understand the underlying causes of the maladaptive behaviour beyond the basic assumption that all behaviour is learned. Where individuals have acquired maladaptive behaviour patterns, these can be unlearned and/or new behaviours learned in their place.

Appropriateness
Strengths
- Behavioural therapies are relatively quick and require little effort from the patient.
- They are successful with simpler disorders which have clear behavioural patterns, for example phobias, obsessive–compulsive and developmental disorders, but less successful with serious disorders which have a substantial genetic component.
- For some disorders it is the only viable option, for example treating those who have suffered brain damage.

Limitations
- The therapies rely on treating the symptoms only, which may result in **symptom**

substitution, where new symptoms replace those that have been unlearned because the underlying problem has not been treated.

- It is not clear whether the reason such therapies are successful is due to conditioning or whether the therapist–client relationship may also be important.
- New behaviours may be learned in the therapist's office but these may not generalise to the real world (**context-dependent learning**). There are ethical questions about manipulating behaviour, especially because the therapist is likely to choose which behaviours are undesirable.

Classical conditioning

Classical conditioning involves learning a new stimulus–response (S–R) link through association (pairing an unconditioned stimulus (UCS) with a neutral stimulus (NS) so that the NS comes to produce the same response as the UCS — a new conditioned response (CR)). Behavioural therapies that are based on classical conditioning work best with behaviours that are difficult to control voluntarily.

Operant conditioning

Operant conditioning involves increasing the probability of a target behaviour by offering rewards (positive or negative reinforcement). Behaviours may decrease in probability if punishment is used. Behavioural therapies that are based on operant conditioning are referred to as **behaviour modification techniques**. These techniques work best with behaviours that are under voluntary control.

Behavioural therapies based on classical conditioning

Aversion therapy

Use

Aversion therapy is used to eradicate undesirable behaviours, such as alcoholism, sexual deviation or homosexuality (advocated in the past by Hans Eysenck and claimed to continue still in, for example, the Navy).

Mode of action

The target behaviour is paired with an aversive stimulus (e.g. an electric shock) so that a new S–R link is learned: the target behaviour no longer elicits a sense of pleasure but instead is associated with an unpleasant experience.

Alcoholics are given a drug that makes them vomit when drinking. Eventually the nausea becomes a conditioned response to the presentation of alcohol (conditioned stimulus). Sexual deviants are given an electric shock when they view socially unacceptable photographs.

Issues surrounding use

Appropriateness

There are obvious ethical concerns about using an unpleasant stimulus. A variation, called **covert sensitisation**, involves the patient simply imagining unpleasant consequences.

Effectiveness

- The therapy may appear to be successful in the short term and also in the context where the learning took place, but when the patient 'knows' that no sickness or shocks will follow the behaviour, then the effects are reduced.
- Smith et al. (1991) found higher abstinence rates after 12 months in alcoholics treated with aversion therapy plus counselling in comparison with those treated with counselling alone (79% compared with 67%). This suggests that such multi-modal programmes may be highly effective.
- Bancroft and Marks (1968) treated 19 males, including three paedophiles, with aversive instrumental conditioning using electric shocks. After 1 year, around half continued to be 'improved'. Cautela (1967) used covert sensitisation with two homosexuals, resulting in changed behaviour.

Systematic desensitisation

Use

Systematic desensitisation (SD) is used to treat phobias and obsessive–compulsive disorder.

Mode of action

Wolpe (1958) proposed that patients should be taken through the following steps:
(1) Learn deep-muscle relaxation.
(2) Construct a hierarchy of increasingly threatening situations.
(3) Starting at the bottom of the hierarchy, imagine each scene in turn while remaining deeply relaxed.
(4) If the patient feels anxious, the image is stopped and relaxation regained.

There are two factors involved in the success of this therapy:

- **counter-conditioning** — the patient learns to pair the feared object/situation with relaxation rather than anxiety
- **reciprocal inhibition** — it is impossible to maintain two incompatible emotional responses simultaneously (anxiety and relaxation)

Issues surrounding use

Appropriateness

Success may not be due to classical conditioning. It may be that the patient overcomes the phobia simply through exposure to the feared stimulus, not relaxation.

SD can be a rather slow therapy; it may be easier to simply expose oneself to the feared stimulus. This preference may depend on individual differences.

Effectiveness

- Wolpe originally reported 90% effectiveness but later results have not been quite so positive.
- Capafons et al. (1998) successfully treated 20 patients for fear of flying. After a programme of SD, these patients displayed less fear in a flight simulator and were more likely to fly than a control group of patients waiting for therapy.

- SD may be more effective when drugs are taken to reduce anxiety. It can also be paired with modelling (see below). Effectiveness may depend on preferred cognitive style.

Flooding and implosion therapy
Use
Flooding and implosion therapy are used in the treatment of phobias.

Mode of action
In flooding, the patient is given maximum exposure to the feared stimulus, which continues until their fear is reduced. Thus the patient learns that the feared stimulus no longer produces a fear response and a new S–R link is acquired.

In implosion therapy, the patient *imagines* the most fearful situation.

Issues surrounding use
Appropriateness
These therapies overcome the problem that once a phobia has been learned, the individual avoids the phobic situation and thus the behaviour cannot be unlearned. Flooding shows the patient that there is no objective basis to the fear.

Virtual reality techniques may be a useful alternative, producing less anxiety.

Effectiveness
- Real-life exposure (flooding) is more effective than implosion but it does involve placing the patient in an intensely anxiety-provoking situation.
- Fear of flying can be treated in a simulator. One company (FAIT) takes patients on a simulated flight that includes ball lightning and a violent landing. Pupil dilation and other ANS responses are checked and poor performance results in more flooding (as negative reinforcement). They claim success.

Behavioural therapies based on operant conditioning

Token economy
Use
Token economy (TE) is a system that allows for systematic reinforcement of desired achievements by offering rewards (tokens) which can be used to acquire other things. It is used in the school system and in families, as well as in mental hospitals.

The tokens are **secondary reinforcers**. A **primary reinforcer** is something such as food, which satisfies primary needs.

Mode of action
A system of selective reinforcement is used to shape behaviour. Individuals are given tokens when they engage in correct/socially desirable behaviours. The tokens can then be exchanged for primary reinforcers, such as food, or privileges, such as visits to the cinema.

Issues surrounding use

Appropriateness

- The effectiveness of tokens may be due to other factors. For instance, such a system might be positively reinforcing for the nursing staff because it improves patient behaviour.
- The use of external rewards may actually destroy intrinsic motivation so that the behaviour is even less likely to transfer to the real world.
- It destroys autonomy (free will) and may make the individual less flexible in coping with new situations.

Effectiveness

- Allyon and Azrin (1968) used token economy with schizophrenic patients. The patients were given tokens for making their beds or combing their hair. The number of chores the patients performed each day increased from about five to over 40.
- McMonagle and Sultana (2002) reviewed three studies in which schizophrenic patients' behaviour had been managed with token economies. Only one study produced positive findings. The conclusion reached was that the token economy approach may have effects on negative symptoms but it is unclear if these results are reproducible, clinically meaningful and maintained beyond the treatment programme.
- Woods et al. (1984) found that there were long-term changes for a token economy system, possibly because newly acquired behaviours then become 'trapped' by other social reinforcers.

Modelling

Use

Modelling is used to treat phobias and in social skills training, such as with bullies, people with autism or children who find it difficult to make friends.

Mode of action

This method is related to social learning theory and is based on observational learning and vicarious reinforcement. If you can get someone with a psychological disorder to observe someone dealing with the same issues in a more productive fashion, the first person will learn by modelling the second.

For phobias, a client first watches the therapist experiencing the phobic situation calmly, then the patient does the same.

For social skills training, live models demonstrate social skills (e.g. negotiating, smiling and giving compliments).

Issues surrounding use

Appropriateness

Modelling has been described as a kinder, gentler form of implosion therapy. It works best when the model is similar to the client. It is also better if some commentary is added to direct the client to the important behaviours to be modelled.

Effectiveness

- Bandura et al. (1969) worked with snake phobia and found that modelling was most effective when working with a live snake rather than a symbolic representation.
- Cooke and Apolloni (1976) used live models to demonstrate social skills (e.g. smiling and giving compliments) to excessively shy or solitary children. The children's social behaviours increased, and included examples that had not been shown by the model.
- Freeman and Adams (1999) compared two programmes for increasing assertiveness in nurses, one of which contained some modelling. The use of modelling was found to enhance the success of the programme.

Synoptic overview

Different explanations or perspectives

Classical and **operant conditioning** as explanations of behaviour can be compared and contrasted with the **social learning approach** (neo-behavioural) and other approaches (provided that such comparison is used effectively).

Demonstrating different methods used

Various methods are used to assess effectiveness, such as dividing a group of prospective patients into two — one half receiving the therapy and the other half asked to wait for their treatment. Comparisons can be made after the first period of treatment.

Relating overarching issues and debates

Ethical issues — behavioural techniques involve control of a patient's behaviour. The key question is, who determines what is desirable behaviour, i.e. who determines the goals of therapy?

Is psychology a science? Behavioural therapy is a highly experimental approach.

Nature and nurture — the behavioural approach supports the nurture position and the therapy is a means of demonstrating the validity of this argument.

Links with other areas of the specification and other disciplines

AS individual differences — assumptions of the behavioural model in terms of its view on treatment.

Alternatives to biological and behavioural therapies

Specification content

Use and mode of action of therapies derived from either the psychodynamic (e.g. psychoanalysis, psychodrama) or cognitive–behavioural (e.g. rational–emotive therapy, stress inoculation therapy) models of abnormality. Issues surrounding the use of such therapies (e.g. appropriateness and effectiveness).

You are given two models to choose from here. There is no need to study both of them as you will only ever be required to discuss one or the other in the examination. In each case, you need to be familiar with two therapies within the model, i.e. two (or more) psychodynamic therapies or two (or more) cognitive–behavioural therapies. You must not study just one psychodynamic and one cognitive–behavioural therapy.

As with the other therapies, you need to be able to describe and evaluate the use and mode of action of all your chosen therapies, and to be able to describe and evaluate the issues surrounding the use of them. You need to be able to compare and contrast them with biological and behavioural therapies, too.

You are required to produce a synoptic response, so some suggestions to help you with this task are included at the end of this topic (see p. 51). Questions will be designed to facilitate this.

As mentioned above, for this topic you have a choice of studying *one* therapy that is an alternative to the biological and behavioural models. This guide only considers cognitive–behavioural therapies. However, you could use psychodynamic therapies instead (e.g. psychoanalysis and psychodrama).

Cognitive–behavioural therapies: general issues

Cognitive–behavioural therapies combine cognitive assumptions with behavioural treatments.
- Cognitive therapy assumes that our behaviour is the result of our appraisal of a situation. Cognition can rule over emotions and behaviour. A cognitive therapist tries to attack the faulty assumptions, beliefs and coping skills of a client.
- Behavioural therapy is based on how reinforcement and punishment can change behaviour. Behavioural therapy helps clients understand and change their behaviour more concretely.

Strengths
- The therapy is effective in disorders that have a cognitive component, such as depression, anxiety disorders and stress management.
- It is effective in the long term because the solution does not just target the immediate problem.

Limitations
- It is only suitable for certain patients — those who are willing to make the necessary effort and who approach life in a more cognitive manner.
- It requires effort and time from the patient. Therapy often involves 'homework'.

Rational emotive therapy or rational emotive behaviour therapy
Use
Rational emotive therapy (RET) or rational emotive behaviour therapy (REBT) is used to treat anxiety, depression, obsessive–compulsive disorders, personality disorders, addictions, eating disorders and clients with poor interpersonal skills.

Mode of action

Ellis (1962) proposed that individuals have irrational, self-defeating belief systems which cause them to react to situations with undesirable emotions such as anxiety or depression. He described this as 'ABC':

A = activating event ⟶ B = beliefs about the activating event ⟶ C = consequences

The cure lies in identifying and challenging these beliefs and replacing them with more rational, positive ones. The therapist is directive and aggressive. Clients are encouraged to take responsibility for their own distress and to identify and then deal with the three core 'musts':

- 'I *must* do well and get approval, or else I'm worthless.'
- 'You *must* treat me reasonably, considerately and lovingly, or else I'm no good.'
- 'Life *must* be fair, easy and hassle-free, or else it's awful.'

Each 'must' leads to unhealthy mental states, such as depression or lack of self-worth. Ellis claims that unconditional self-acceptance (USA) is a vital outcome of the therapy and a major goal is to help people 'unwhiningly accept' life circumstances.

Issues surrounding use

Appropriateness

REBT is probably more suitable for some personality types than others, such as those who feel guilty because of their own perceived inadequacies and who generally impose high demands on themselves (Brandsma et al., 1978).

Effectiveness

- Corey (1996) reviewed 47 outcome studies and found that 31 had significant findings in favour of REBT, and that in all studies REBT was the most effective form of therapy.
- Therapists often use an eclectic combination of methods which makes it hard to evaluate REBT alone. A further problem is that the goals set by the therapist determine the effectiveness of the therapy.

Cognitive restructuring therapy (or cognitive therapy)

Use

Cognitive restructuring therapy is used in the treatment of depression, anxiety disorders, eating disorders, stress, bereavement, relationship problems and, possibly, schizophrenia.

Mode of action

Beck (1976) used the **cognitive triad** to describe the unrealistic, negative beliefs depressed clients hold about themselves, the world and the future. Depressed clients typically regard themselves as helpless and worthless; they interpret events in the world in a negative and defeatist way, and they see the future as hopeless because their worthlessness will prevent any improvement occurring in their situation.

First, the therapist and the client agree on what the problem is and then set goals for therapy (**collaborative empiricism**). Second, the therapist challenges the client's self-defeating assumptions, and asks the client to practise more positive behaviours between sessions (emphasising both cognitions and behaviour). Clients are also asked to compare their beliefs with reality to highlight the unrealistic nature of these beliefs. For example, the client might be asked to keep a record of insulting comments so that the therapist can demonstrate how beliefs do not match reality.

Issues surrounding use

Appropriateness

The therapy is relatively short (compared with traditional methods of psychotherapy). Typically it involves about 15 sessions, which minimises the cost. Most patients experience positive changes in approximately 12–15 sessions.

Cognitive therapy emphasises many practical strategies that can be used to help the client cope with life more effectively, even when the therapy is over.

Effectiveness

- Hollon et al. (1988) found greater improvement in depressed patients who were given cognitive restructuring therapy than in those receiving drug therapy. There was some evidence of relapse in the 'drug only' group over the next 2 years but not in the other patients.
- Beck and Rector (1998) claim that schizophrenic patients who are treated using cognitive restructuring therapy in addition to drugs have improved as much as 50% more than those receiving drugs alone. These treatment gains exceed those produced by alternative psychosocial interventions, such as befriending, problem-solving and supportive counselling.

Stress inoculation therapy (SIT)

Use

SIT involves dealing with stress by preparing someone to be better able to cope. It can be likened to a form of vaccination.

Mode of action

Meichenbaum (1975) proposed three main phases to this process:

(1) *Conceptualisation phase* — the client is taught to understand stress better and to view perceived threats as problems to be solved. This enables the client to reconceptualise the problem.

(2) *Skills acquisition phase (and rehearsal)* — coping skills (e.g. relaxation, methods of attention diversion and time management) and coping self-statements (e.g. 'Don't worry — worry won't help anything') are taught and practised in the clinic and then rehearsed in real life. The skills taught are both cognitive and behavioural: cognitive because they encourage the client to think in a different way and behavioural because they involve learning new behaviours through rewards (conditioning).

(3) *Application phase (and follow-through)* — clients are given opportunities to apply the newly learned coping skills in different situations. Various techniques may be used, such as imagining how to deal with stressful situations, modelling and role playing. Booster sessions (follow-through) are offered later.

Issues surrounding use

Appropriateness

The focus on skills acquisition provides long-lasting effectiveness. Skills are taught, practised and followed through.

Effectiveness

- Meichenbaum (1977) compared SIT with desensitisation in clients learning to deal with their snake phobia. Meichenbaum found that both forms of therapy reduced the phobia but that SIT was better because it helped clients deal with a second, non-treated phobia. This shows that SIT can inoculate against future stressful situations as well as offering help in coping with current problems.
- Fontana et al. (1999) assessed a peer-led stress inoculation programme in college students. After a six-session treatment programme, the participants had lower heart rates and lower anxiety levels than did controls. This difference was maintained at a 6-month follow-up.

Synoptic overview

Different explanations or perspectives

The **cognitive–behavioural approach** can be evaluated through a comparison with other approaches, provided that such comparison is used effectively.

Within the cognitive–behavioural approach, there are various different therapies that count as different perspectives and can also be compared and contrasted.

Relating overarching issues and debates

Ethical issues relating to the treatment of mental illness.

Links with other areas of the specification and other disciplines

AS individual differences — assumptions of the psychodynamic and cognitive models of abnormality in terms of their views on treatment.

Broad issues of psychological concern

Reliability and **validity** are issues for all therapies.

General commentary on evaluating effectiveness

- Seligman (1975) reported that a survey of all psychotherapies found that no single psychotherapy did any better than any other for any problem. He concluded that these results confirm the 'dodo bird' hypothesis — that all forms of psychotherapy do about equally well (Luborsky et al., 1975).
- It is difficult to compare effectiveness when each therapy has its own goal and uses different outcome measures. How does one assess effectiveness or 'cure'? It depends how one defines the problem.
- All therapies may share common factors, which may explain the success of a particular therapy. For example, Sloane et al. (1975) found that patients indicated that very similar factors were responsible for the success of both behaviour and insight-oriented therapies, such as the therapist's personality and being able to talk to a sympathetic person.

- Most treatments actually use several therapies jointly. Therefore, it is impossible to assess the effectiveness of any one therapy.
- Individuals and illnesses can respond differently to a particular therapy. This means that there are no universally successful therapies.
- It is not always easy to assess effectiveness. For example, in the 'hello–goodbye effect', patients overestimate disorder at the start of treatment to elicit care and underestimate symptoms at the end to show appreciation for help.
- The apparent effectiveness of a therapy may be due to selective publication of trial results and misleading statistics, for example not including findings from participants who dropped out.

Questions
&
Answers

This section contains sample questions in the style of Unit 5. Each is accompanied by a full explanation of the question's requirements, followed by a candidate's response.

Examiner's comments

All candidate responses are followed by examiner's comments. These are preceded by the icon *e*, and indicate where credit is due. In the weaker answers, they point out areas for improvement, specific problems and common errors such as poor time management, lack of clarity, weak or non-existent development, irrelevance, mis-interpretation of the question and mistaken meanings of terms.

The comments also indicate how each example answer would have been marked in an actual exam, using the criteria listed on page 6.

Classificatory systems

Discuss research (theories *and/or* studies) into the reliability and validity of classificatory systems for mental illness.

(30 marks)

The issues of reliability and validity are named in this part of the specification, which means that you can be asked a question specifically on these topics. Such issues are synoptic because they are psychology-wide concerns rather than simply being specific to this section.

The injunction 'discuss' is an AO1 and AO2 term requiring you to describe (AO1) and evaluate (AO2) the named issues. If you only discuss reliability or validity, this would be seen as partial performance with a ceiling of 9/15 marks for AO1 and 9/15 marks for AO2. In this essay, you would not gain credit for describing classificatory systems (i.e. *DSM* and *ICD*), nor for any general evaluations of these systems. You should describe the reliability and validity of *DSM*, *ICD* and/or any other classificatory system, and comment on the issues. Rosenhan's classic study may be used as a form of commentary/evaluation.

Note that the term 'research' refers to theories and/or studies. Therefore, AO1 credit can be given for describing theoretical approaches or for descriptions of studies.

Answer to question 1: A-grade candidate

Two of the most important issues related to classificatory systems are reliability and validity. The concept of reliability refers to the extent to which any classificatory system will produce the same classification if used by the same clinician on different occasions or, more importantly, when used by different clinicians. Any tool used in measurement needs to be reliable (e.g. a ruler or psychological test). Classificatory systems are used to measure psychological disorder and thus are a tool of measurement.

The concept of validity refers to the trueness of something, i.e. whether a classificatory system produces an outcome representing something real. We can assess validity in various ways. An important way is in terms of causation (aetiological validity). If we can identify a single cause (aetiology means cause), such as a particular virus, then this makes the validity of the disorder high. This is rare in mental disorders but was the case for general paresis, a mental disorder due to syphilis.

A second way to assess validity is descriptive validity. The symptoms for any one condition should be distinct. In other words, when a patient presents with a particular set of symptoms, it should be clear that these represent one rather than several possible disorders. If the symptoms overlap, then the syndromes lack validity. Eysenck (1997) claims that validity is low for *DSM* because many patients actually have several disorders at once. For example, many patients with one anxiety disorder also have a second anxiety disorder.

There is also predictive validity. The main aim of classification is to be able to prescribe a suitable form of treatment once a diagnosis has been made and also to be able to predict the course of the illness.

The classic study by Rosenhan (1973) illustrates both a lack of reliability and validity of classificatory systems. In this study, Rosenhan arranged for eight normal individuals to act as potential patients. They each told a psychiatrist that they were hearing voices; seven were diagnosed as schizophrenic and admitted to a mental hospital. The fact that normal individuals could be so easily misdiagnosed challenges the validity of the classificatory scheme. The classificatory system cannot be very good or valid if such an error was made.

In a further study, Rosenhan sought to see if similar mistakes could be made in the other direction (classifying the insane as sane). This time he told psychiatrists that some pseudopatients would be seeking admission to their hospital. There were in fact no pseudopatients but a large number of actual patients were confidently labelled pseudopatients by some psychiatrists, again challenging the validity of classification. There was also poor agreement among clinicians, demonstrating low reliability.

It is worth noting that classificatory systems have been improved since the time of these studies and current revisions claim quite high inter-rater reliability (e.g. over 0.9 for schizophrenia). The diagnosis of physical disorders is often no better than this. Validity, however, continues to be uncertain and Rosenhan's findings are disquieting, especially when one considers the effect of such a diagnosis. Once labelled schizophrenic it may be hard to escape from this, unlike suffering from a physical condition where much less stigma is attached. This makes validity a more serious issue for classification and diagnosis of mental disorders.

The findings should not be accepted without some challenge. First, the original patients were actually discharged quite rapidly in contrast with usual lengthy hospitalisations for 'true' patients. This suggests that they weren't truly classified as schizophrenic. Second, the pseudopatient paradigm acted as a demand characteristic and may not be representative of real life.

Rosenhan's research raises serious ethical questions. Psychiatrists were deceived in both studies and also some true patients may have not been diagnosed in the second study. The question is one of ends and means. Is the importance of the findings sufficient to justify the means?

Perhaps the key problem of validity raised in Rosenhan's study is that the differences between normal and abnormal behaviour are not that great. For example, Rachman and de Silva (1978) found that over half of 'normal' people have similar compulsions to those found in individuals diagnosed as obsessive–compulsive. Mental illness is a matter of degree, not all-or-nothing conditions, which makes validity hard to establish. Many clinical characteristics are related to time, for example depression is diagnosed when symptoms have occurred daily for more than 2 weeks.

A further issue to consider is cultural, social and gender biases. In order to make a valid diagnosis, there should be no biases, yet more women are diagnosed with depression, more working-class people are diagnosed with schizophrenia, and more West Indians are diagnosed with schizophrenia. There are various explanations for such biases, but most importantly, it is probably because classificatory systems are based on white, middle-class, male standards of behaviour.

If classificatory systems are regarded as unreliable and lacking validity, what alternatives are there? One possibility is to take a more idiographic approach, i.e. one where the unique characteristics of the individual case are focused on. Each patient is analysed individually and no generalisations are made. This is an unusual approach and one that has the disadvantage that causes of mental disorder cannot be identified. The nomothetic (statistical) approach enables us to identify syndromes and physical causes, as in the case of general paresis, and this may also be increasingly true for schizophrenia. It may be desirable to combine both approaches.

e The essay begins with explanations (AO1) of the two concepts — reliability and validity — and then moves on to describe how validity of classificatory systems is achieved. This discussion has both reasonable depth (detail) and breadth (covering different kinds of validity). Rosenhan's study is used to illustrate both validity and reliability and could be credited as AO1 or AO2, but since the essay is short on AO1 material it would attract most marks by being considered as such. Note how the candidate resists the temptation to provide a lengthy description of the study and instead restricts the account to the relevant details.

The rest of the essay assesses Rosenhan's study and then broadens to consider other issues related to validity. The coverage of synoptic possibilities is enhanced through this commentary (ethics; cultural, social and gender biases; and nomothetic versus idiographic approaches).

AO1: description of validity and reliability is slightly limited. It is accurate and reasonably detailed. There is increasing evidence of depth and breadth — more depth than breadth in terms of content and synoptic possibilities. The organisation and structure are coherent. The AO1 content is worth 11 marks out of 15.

AO2: credit is achieved through consideration of the problems related to reliability and validity. Material has been used effectively and there is evidence of both appropriate selection and coherent elaboration. To demonstrate a greater sense of 'thoroughness', the candidate might have made reference to specific studies, such as when discussing gender bias in depression. For AO2, 13 marks out of 15 are awarded.

e **This essay scores a total of 24 marks out of 30.**

Question 2

Multiple-personality disorder

(a) Describe *two or more* case studies of multiple-personality disorder. (15 marks)

(b) Assess the extent to which multiple-personality disorder is an iatrogenic phenomenon. (15 marks)

> In this two-part question, all of the AO1 marks are in part (a). This means that any evaluation of case studies would receive no credit in part (a); nor would it receive credit in part (b), as that is not the evaluation that is required.
>
> In part (b) you are required to consider whether or not multiple-personality disorder is something 'created' by a therapist. As this part of the question is entirely AO2, no credit would be awarded for description. However, it is important to use your time appropriately. Part (b) is worth half the marks for the question and therefore you should put half your time into this and not spend further time on description. It is better to spend time thinking about the question and simply write less, but relevant, material.
>
> A well-balanced answer will consider both possibilities, i.e. that it is iatrogenic or, alternatively, that it is spontaneous. However, there is no penalty for presenting only one side of the argument.

■ ■ ■

Answer to question 2: A-grade candidate

(a) The best known case study of MPD is *The Three Faces of Eve*. In this case, a woman, known as Eve White, was referred to a psychiatrist because of frequent headaches. One day, during a consultation, she went silent and quite a different personality emerged who was called Eve Black. She was wicked and didn't feel she had to be good to anyone. She had little time for Eve White's child and husband. When both Eves were given psychological tests, some differences emerged in terms of IQ and memory.

When Eve White was young and her sister was born, Eve felt very jealous. She remained a good girl but it may be that at this time her personality fragmented to cope with her negative feelings. Eve Black embodied these and enabled Eve White to remain nice to her family. During therapy, a third personality, Jane, emerged. Eventually, a number of others emerged and now the real Eve, Chris Sizemore, has managed to reintegrate herself.

Another well-known case study is Sybil. She was treated by a psychiatrist because she was disturbed and, during therapy, a number of different personalities emerged, including a baby and several men. Sybil claimed to have been abused when she was younger, which might explain her MPD.

Another case study is Jonah, who had headaches like Eve. He was observed in hospital and it was noticed that his personality sometimes became distinctly different. There appeared to be four different personalities, each playing a useful role and contributing to the whole personality. One was the sensible, rational person; another was the ladies' man; a third was the protector; and Jonah was the central figure. Each personality had emerged as a response to some event in Jonah's childhood.

@ This answer provides accurate and reasonably detailed coverage of three case histories. The accounts are somewhat abrupt and none is given in enough depth or breadth to be considered 'substantial', especially in the case of the second two case studies. Therefore, this is a slightly limited account. Synopticity is represented here by the variety of case studies, but is slightly limited. This part is awarded 11 marks out of 15.

(b) There has been a huge increase in the number of MPD cases since that of Eve, which raises the question of whether such cases are real mental disorders or whether the apparent illness has been manufactured in some way by the therapist. When a patient is hypnotised, it may be quite easy to 'suggest' alternative personalities, a concept then readily taken up by the patient. This has been claimed to be the case for Sybil. In recent years, a psychiatrist reviewed tape recordings of Sybil and her therapist which suggest that the 'alters' were not spontaneous but were responses to suggestions made by the therapist. It may even be that the therapist was doing this knowingly and fraudulently in an effort to attract attention.

Ken Bianchi used MPD as a way of trying to escape blame for a series of horrible murders. He invented alters but this wasn't a case of iatrogenic cause because he did it knowingly and by himself. It was not communicated by a therapist.

This view is supported by a study in Switzerland (Modestin) which found most of the cases of MPD were attributed to only three psychiatrists. In other words, some psychiatrists are overdiagnosing the condition, which could be explained by the fact that they are in some way conveying expectations to their patients and creating the disorder in suggestible individuals.

Spanos et al. (1985) conducted an experiment which further supports this view. Participants were asked to pretend that they were an accused murderer and were hypnotised. In addition, members of one group were told that a part of their personality might want to communicate with the 'therapist' whereas those in another group were not given this suggestion. Not surprisingly, those in the first group were much more likely to invent another personality. It may be that this finding is due to role play, but Spanos takes the view that hypnotism generally and MPD in particular are social constructions in which the individual learns to exhibit certain behaviours in order to play a social role. It could be that MPD is a culture-bound disorder where the condition may be real but the way of expressing the disorder has been created by expectations common in our society.

There are arguments against this. It may be that some cases of MPD are iatrogenic, but not all. Not all MPD patients have been hypnotised and therefore suggestion through hypnosis cannot be used to explain all cases. It would be hard to explain the case of Eve in this way because the idea was new to her and her therapists.

question

e The case for iatrogenesis is presented well here. Evidence is identified and used effectively to demonstrate that the disorders may be manufactured. Most of these arguments are elaborated, though the second paragraph, for example, lacks thorough explanations. There is no requirement for a balanced answer, but for top marks one would expect more than the brief final paragraph as a counterpoint. This part is worth 11 marks out of 15.

e **The total awarded for this question is 22 marks out of 30.**

Culture-bound syndromes

Critically consider arguments *for* the existence of culture-bound syndromes. (30 marks)

> The injunction 'critically consider' requires both AO1 (description) and AO2 (evaluation). In the context of this question, it means that you must describe and then offer an evaluation of the relevant arguments. This may involve presenting a counter-argument or an examination of evidence. Either way, AO2 credit is awarded only when material has been explicitly used as evaluation. Simply describing a counter-argument is not evaluation.

■ ■ ■

Answer to question 3: C-grade candidate

A culture-bound syndrome is a particular sort of mental illness. It is a recurrent, locality-specific pattern of behaviour. It is a mental disorder that exists in one culture but not in another. Or so it is claimed. But is it true? Are there such things as culture-bound syndromes?

There are case studies that support this view. Koro is an illness that is found in Asia. The symptoms are that the individual, almost exclusively male, believes that his genitals will retract into his body and possibly lead to death. The victim also experiences high levels of general anxiety. It may be that some people in other cultures experience koro, which would make it not culture-bound, but it has been argued that such cases are koro-like states and not true koro. A koro-like state is when a set of similar symptoms is exhibited while suffering another mental disorder. Such cases are difficult to treat because the symptoms are related to severe mental illness, whereas koro is relatively easy to treat. However, it has been suggested that our own cultural myth that masturbation leads to blindness might be linked to koro (because it is a fear related to sexuality), so this would mean that koro is not culture-specific.

There are also arguments about whether anorexia is a culture-bound condition. Eating disorders are much more common in the West, which may be related to the way that the media represent attractiveness. This means that the symptoms are culture-bound but the disorder is not. An individual who is prone to anxiety may express this disorder by not eating. If that individual were living in another culture, she or he might exhibit different symptoms. This means that it is not a true culture-bound syndrome because the real underlying condition is universal and found worldwide; it is just the symptoms that are bound to one culture.

In one study in Hong Kong it was reported that eating disorders were on the increase. This may be because of increased exposure to Western media, resulting in young people learning new ways of behaving to express their anxieties.

Another possible culture-bound syndrome is amok. This is again found in Asia where individuals run amok. They act in a wild and aggressive manner for a short period of time. They may attack others and even kill themselves. Similar cases have been documented in this country, such as the murderous attack at Dunblane where one man shot a room full of schoolchildren. We even use the term 'amok' to describe this behaviour.

There are lots of these syndromes and many are now listed in the *DSM*. There is also brain fag, zar, pibloktoq and dhat. They are all different from other syndromes as they are specific to certain cultures and are not just symptoms of an underlying condition such as anxiety.

The issue of culture-bound syndromes is important for the science of diagnosis because errors can easily be made and true illnesses may be misdiagnosed if they are expressed differently in different cultures. For example, a psychiatrist might think that someone who was hearing voices had schizophrenia whereas hearing voices was normal in that person's own culture. Alternatively, someone might complain that he was afraid that his genitals were retracting into his body and be diagnosed as insane, whereas he was in fact suffering from a culture-specific syndrome that requires a specific treatment. This is an ethical issue related to culture bias. There is also gender bias in diagnosis.

e It seems that this candidate has a good grasp of the concept of CBSs but has insufficient knowledge to present a grade-A response. Strictly speaking, the candidate has not answered the question directly but, instead, has presented information (case studies) about CBSs and then extracted arguments related to the existence of these syndromes. This results in a lack of structure. Counter-arguments have been used effectively, however. The final paragraph is a general assessment of the concept and importance of understanding CBSs. This contributes to synopticity by addressing issues such as culture bias in diagnosis and ethics. The AO1 content is quite detailed and reasonably constructed, but limited. It is worth 8 out of 15 marks. AO2 commentary is again limited and not always used effectively. It is slightly less impressive than the AO1 material, and is awarded 7 out of 15 marks.

e **A total of 15 marks out of 30 is awarded, which is equivalent to a grade C.**

Schizophrenia

(a) Outline the clinical characteristics of schizophrenia. (5 marks)

(b) Critically consider biological explanations of schizophrenia. (25 marks)

The first part of this question asks for the clinical characteristics of schizophrenia. Not all questions on this topic *do* require these, so only include them if, like here, they are requested explicitly. There are a number of different ways that you could outline the 'clinical characteristics' of schizophrenia (e.g. different types) but the symptoms are the most obvious way of doing this. A little mental arithmetic would help here. 5 marks is one-sixth of the total marks for this question; therefore, one-sixth of the time (about 6–7 minutes) should be spent on this part.

As the first part of the question uses up 5 of the 15 marks available for AO1 in this question, that leaves 10 marks of AO1 and 15 marks of AO2 in the second part. You should therefore bias your answer to part (b) slightly more towards evaluation than description. The question asks for *biological* explanations of schizophrenia. Two points should be emphasised here. First, any mention of *psychological* explanations should be part of a sustained critical evaluation of biological explanations rather than alternative explanations. Second, synoptic credit will be enhanced by the range of explanations and methods you choose to include. General credit will also be enhanced by the extent to which your response is well-structured, so make a plan in advance of writing the essay, outlining what you are going to cover.

■ ■ ■

Answer to question 4: A-grade candidate

(a) The positive symptoms of schizophrenia are those that make themselves known by their presence. They include thought disorder, hallucinations and delusions. Thought disorders involve irrational thinking. Schizophrenics cannot organise their thoughts well and often jump from topic to topic. The most common hallucinations in schizophrenia are auditory. Typically, schizophrenics hear voices talking to them. Schizophrenics may also suffer delusions of persecution or of grandeur.

The negative symptoms of schizophrenia are those that involve an absence of normal behaviour. They include disturbances in emotion, motor control and social functioning. Some schizophrenics display no emotions at all; others may display inappropriate emotional reactions. Schizophrenics may display unusual physical actions such as giggling and laughing, or standing immobile for hours at a time.

There is a clear distinction in this answer between positive and negative symptoms. This is a good idea, and helps to order the symptoms that follow. The main examples of positive and negative symptoms are given and these have sufficient detail to warrant the full 5 marks for this part of the question.

(b) Excessive activity of the neurotransmitter dopamine has been linked to schizophrenia. In schizophrenics, neurones that use dopamine fire too often and transmit too many messages; as a result, the symptoms associated with schizophrenia appear. Evidence for the role of dopamine comes from two main sources. Antipsychotic drugs that reduce the symptoms of schizophrenia block receptor sites for dopamine, and therefore reduce its activity.

Levels of dopamine in the brain can be assessed from levels of HVA, a chemical by-product of dopamine. By measuring concentrations of HVA in the brain, it has been found that schizophrenic patients have much higher levels of dopamine than do normal controls. Autopsies of the brains of schizophrenic patients have also shown that they have far more dopamine receptors than do non-schizophrenics.

A major problem for the dopamine hypothesis is that only around two-thirds of schizophrenic patients respond to traditional antipsychotic drugs that block the receptor sites for dopamine. The introduction of 'atypical' antipsychotics such as clozapine has a beneficial effect for those patients who do not respond to traditional drugs. Clozapine acts only weakly on dopamine receptors but acts on receptors for serotonin too, suggesting that, for some people at least, serotonin may also be implicated in schizophrenia.

Since the 1970s, there has been increasing evidence for the presence of brain damage in some people diagnosed with schizophrenia. It is believed that brain damage is associated with negative symptoms rather than positive symptoms. On the basis of this, Crow (1980) suggested that there are two distinct forms of the disorder, Type A (positive symptoms and no brain damage) and Type B (negative symptoms and evidence of brain damage).

This classification is supported by the fact that traditional drug therapies tend to be more successful with Type A schizophrenics than with Type B schizophrenics. The most consistent findings relating to brain damage have come from postmortems, and from CT and MRI studies, which have shown enlarged ventricles (suggesting atrophy in surrounding tissues) in the limbic system. In turn, these large ventricles are associated with poor performance on neuropsychological tests, and a poor response to drug treatment.

Schizophrenia appears to be heritable, which is good evidence for it being a biological disorder. Adoption studies (e.g. Kety et al., 1968) and twin studies (e.g. Gottesman and Shields, 1976) have supported a genetic link. However, it does not appear to be caused by a single gene, as less than 50% of the children whose parents are both schizophrenic have the disorder. It is possible, therefore, that the disorder is caused by the influence of several genes, or that individuals develop a vulnerability to schizophrenia which may or may not develop in later life.

The diathesis–stress explanation suggests that individuals may have a predisposition (a 'diathesis') towards developing schizophrenia, which then makes them more vulnerable to later environmental events (stress). It is fairly well established that schizophrenia involves an inherited predisposition that makes some people more likely to develop the disorder than others, but whether they develop schizophrenia or not may be determined by the later difficulties that they face in life.

Statistical studies of hereditary relationships have been criticised on a number of points, which include the unreliability of diagnosis of schizophrenia and the lack of control of variables such as socioeconomic class and other environmental factors. While genetics has been implicated in schizophrenia, environmental factors are believed to be involved as well. Even if a set of schizophrenia genes is discovered, it will not mean that a person with the genes will automatically develop the mental illness. Rather, it means that the person has an increased risk of developing schizophrenia. The fact that there is less than 100% concordance for schizophrenia in monozygotic twins cannot be ignored in considering genetic influences in schizophrenia. Recent studies of monozygotic twins that have used improved sampling and research techniques have found significantly lower concordance rates for schizophrenia than earlier studies. We may conclude, therefore, that genetic factors are implicated in the development of schizophrenia. However, though necessary, they alone are not sufficient conditions for the development of this disorder.

e This is a well-structured and clearly planned response to this part of the question. There is just the right amount of AO1 material (slightly less than the AO2) and every description is accurate and well-detailed. There are three clear strands to this essay: neurotransmitter activity (the dopamine hypothesis), brain dysfunction and genetics. Each of these is understood by the candidate, and the answer as a whole forms a clear and coherent account. The research evidence is carefully integrated into the answer so that it forms a key part of the overall evaluation, rather than simply being another aspect of the descriptive content. All the evaluation is highly effective, so this response is worth a creditable 10 marks for the AO1 component of this question, and 15 marks for the AO2 component.

e **Overall, 30 marks out of 30 are awarded.**

Depression

Discuss psychological explanations of depression. (30 marks)

Unlike the previous question, this one does not require a description of the clinical characteristics of the disorder, so any such inclusion is a waste of time and effort. The use of the word 'discuss' in the question indicates that you need to both describe (AO1) and evaluate (AO2) your explanations. The use of the plural 'explanations' also alerts you to the fact that more than one is needed. There is no clear answer to the question 'how many explanations is best?' You score more marks by including a spread of explanations but then again you need to add sufficient detail, so a compromise position between breadth and depth is the best solution.

■ ■ ■

Answer to question 5: B-grade candidate

DSM-IV describes the symptoms of depression as being sad, with a depressed mood, plus at least four other symptoms, which include the following:

- loss of interest in usual activities
- difficulties in sleeping
- poor appetite and weight loss
- loss of energy
- feelings of worthlessness and guilt
- thoughts of suicide

Some psychologists, such as Beck, believe that irrational ideas cause depression. Depressed people are more likely to think in ways that could make them feel sad and depressed. For example, if things have gone badly in the past, they may conclude that the future will be just as bad. Some critics suggest that depressed people actually don't think much about the future because it has little meaning for them, or is threatening in some way. Dwelling on the future may also lead to suicidal thoughts and the belief that things simply won't get better (even if this is an erroneous belief). This hopeless vision of the future is based on a belief that their problems are too large, too many and unsolvable.

The theory of learned helplessness (Seligman, 1965) explains depression by saying that depressed people learn to be helpless. They learn through experience that whatever they do is a waste of time because they cannot escape from whatever is causing them stress. Over the course of their lives, depressed people learn that they have no control over things that happen to them. They also tend to make different attributions about their behaviour compared with other people. Whereas non-depressives tend to use a 'self-serving' bias to explain away failure in their life (as not being their fault, but bad luck or someone else's fault), depressives tend to do the opposite, seeing failure as very much their fault.

Some critics believe that these sad feelings exist before the depressive thoughts. In other words, events or physiological factors lead to negative thinking patterns rather than the other way around. Others believe that emotions and thoughts are independent of each other and that irrational behaviour is caused by how we feel rather than irrational thoughts. In spite of these criticisms, however, cognitive explanations are the most accepted explanations of depression.

Psychoanalysts believe that depression develops out of early interactions with parents. During the Electra conflict, a young girl 'discovers' that she has been castrated by her mother. She feels anger towards the mother but is powerless to do anything about it. This anger towards the mother is turned against herself in a form of self-hatred and this causes depression. Because of their feelings of loss (part of penis envy), women are more vulnerable to depression than men. However, psychoanalytic explanations are criticised for being unparsimonious — they are unnecessarily complicated. A simpler explanation of why women are more likely to develop depression compared with men is that women are more likely to seek medical help for their depression whereas men find other ways of dealing with their depression, like denial or alcoholism. Supporting this claim is the fact that although women outnumber men two to one in terms of depression, the opposite is true for alcoholism.

A final explanation of depression is the role of life events such as bereavement. Brown and Harris (1965) found that women who had lost their 'close, confiding relationship' (usually their mother) were more vulnerable to depression following significant life events such as bereavement or a serious illness. Research has suggested that life events such as divorce can trigger depression, but some critics argue that the direction of this relationship is not proven, as the depressed person may have contributed to his/her own divorce rather than the other way around.

A problem with all psychological explanations of depression is that they ignore all the evidence from physiology. If Prozac didn't work, why would people take it?

e This is a generally competent answer to the question, showing a good understanding of a range of different psychological explanations of depression. The description of the cognitive perspective on depression is fairly well detailed, although the evaluation is brief. The treatment of learned helplessness and its related material on attributional styles is much better but, as with the cognitive perspective, AO2 material is not developed well. Research support would have added to the AO2 component considerably, and this is probably what stands between this answer and a grade A. The answer ends with a good, balanced discussion of psychoanalytic ideas on depression which is rich in both AO1 and AO2. This earns a creditable 11 marks (slightly limited) for the AO1 component of the question and 8 marks (limited) for the AO2 component.

e **Overall, a total of 19 out of 30 marks is awarded.**

Anxiety disorders

Compare and contrast biological and psychological explanations for any *one* anxiety disorder.

(30 marks)

e This is not an easy question for those who are under-prepared. The 'compare and contrast' injunction requires a description of biological and psychological explanations for any one anxiety disorder. This is the AO1 component of the question. However, unlike most of the other questions we have looked at, the AO2 component is not a simple evaluation of these explanations. It requires comparisons (i.e. showing similarities) *and* contrasts (i.e. showing the differences) between biological and psychological explanations.

■ ■ ■

Answer to question 6: A-grade candidate

Unlike other anxiety disorders, which are typically triggered by objects or situations that most people would not find threatening, situations that cause post-traumatic stress disorders (PTSD) would be traumatic for anyone. Recent studies have shown that childhood events seem to leave some people vulnerable to developing post-traumatic stress disorders in response to later traumatic experiences. People whose childhoods have been characterised by poverty, whose family members suffered mental disorders or who experienced assault or abuse at an early age are more likely to develop PTSD in the face of later trauma than are people without such childhood experiences (Kolb, 1992).

However, whereas psychological research has focused mainly on identifying factors that put exposed individuals at 'risk' (e.g. previous trauma exposure), more recent data show that the risk of PTSD may be influenced more by genetic make-up and family environment. For example, studies show an increased prevalence of PTSD in the adult children of Holocaust survivors, even though these children as a group did not have greater exposure to life-threatening events.

It has been suggested that the tendency of many abused children to dissociate themselves from the experience and memory of abuse may become a habitual way of dealing with traumatic events in life. This leads them to 'wall off' later traumas too and sets the stage for the development of PTSD (Bremner, 1993). Other studies suggest that people with certain personality profiles are more likely to develop these disorders. It has been found, for example, that rape victims who had psychological problems before they were assaulted, and war veterans who had poor relationships before they went into combat, run a risk of developing prolonged stress reactions after traumatic experiences.

Biological explanations, in contrast, have stressed the importance of neuro-physiological differences in those who are more vulnerable to PTSD. Veterans of the Vietnam War with PTSD have been found to have higher levels of cortico-trophin releasing factor, which may be the reason behind their high anxiety and fear-related behaviours. Biological explanations play down the role of early experience and emphasise instead the importance of genetics in the development of PTSD. In one study of Vietnam war veterans (Reich et al., 1996), which compared the family histories of probands with PTSD and probands with other anxiety disorders, researchers found a much higher incidence of PTSD in the family histories of PTSD probands than in any of the other groups.

The idea that personality is related in some way to vulnerability to PTSD is supported by research by Kobasa (1990) who discovered that many people respond to stress with a set of positive attitudes that she collectively referred to as hardiness. These help people to carry on their lives with a sense of fortitude, control and commitment. Those who show fewer traits of hardiness show less ability to deal with traumatic events in such a constructive way. It has also been shown that people who are helped by strong social support systems (e.g. family and friends) after a traumatic event are less likely to develop an extended disorder such as PTSD. In contrast, research has shown that weak social support networks have contributed to the development of PTSD in, for example, Vietnam war veterans (Figley and Leventman, 1990).

Biological explanations do not necessarily offer a completely different explanation of PTSD but may add a different level of explanation to psychological reactions. Typical symptoms of PTSD include a state of autonomic hyperarousal and an enhanced startle reaction. A number of biological factors have been linked to such PTSD symptoms. It has been claimed that they make people with PTSD hyper-responsive to stressful stimuli, especially stimuli that are reminiscent of the trauma (Ray, 2002). High levels of adrenaline and noradrenaline in PTSD patients are consistent with a chronic stress reaction. In keeping with the enhanced secretion of these stress hormones, patients with PTSD show an enhanced startle response and higher heart rates and blood pressure. In another study (Southwick et al., 1993), stimulating the noradrenergic part of the nervous system caused flashbacks and panic attacks in PTSD patients but not in controls.

🖉 This answer shows how the two perspectives presented earlier in this unit guide might be used together to provide a compare-and-contrast response. In answering this difficult question, most of the material is used to contrast the two perspectives; however, this need not detract from the overall quality of the response. For AO1, there is plenty of breadth and depth, which is slightly limited because of the lack of empirical studies. The material is accurate and well detailed, and receives 13 out of 15 marks. For AO2, the biological explanations are used largely to provide a counterpoint to the psychological explanations, while at times serving the equally useful function of providing a physiological explanation for observed behaviour patterns. However, just saying 'in contrast' does not guarantee a consideration of similarities or differences. For higher marks, the candidate should have considered more clearly what is similar/different. In addition, a greater range of comparisons should have been made. 9 AO2 marks are awarded.

🖉 **Overall, 22 marks out of 30 are awarded.**

uestion 7

Biological (somatic) therapies

(a) Describe the use and mode of action of *two or more* biological (somatic) therapies. (15 marks)

(b) Evaluate the use of biological (somatic) therapies. (15 marks)

In this question, the AO1 and AO2 components are separated into part (a) (describe — AO1) and part (b) (evaluate — AO2). In part (a) you can gain full marks if you cover two biological therapies. There is no requirement to describe more than two therapies, but the option is there. Candidates who describe only one therapy would receive a partial performance penalty of a maximum of 9 out of 15 marks. The more therapies you cover (increasing breadth), the less detail (depth) you will have time for. In order to maximise your marks, you should aim to achieve a good balance between depth and breadth. Any evaluation offered in part (a) may be exported by the examiner to part (b), although it is best to maintain the coherence of the essay by focusing on description only in part (a). If you spend time on writing evaluation in part (a), less time is available for description and this may affect your AO1 mark.

In part (b) you can offer evaluation of any biological therapies, including those not described in part (a). You may also use other therapies (e.g. behavioural) as a means of evaluation but make sure you do this as part of a sustained critical commentary. A well-balanced response would consider both strengths and weaknesses of the therapies, but there is no requirement to do this.

■ ■ ■

Answer to question 7: A-grade candidate

(a) There are three main forms of biological therapy. The first is ECT (electroconvulsive therapy). An individual is given an anaesthetic and muscle relaxant prior to being given a mild electric shock (about 100 volts) to one or both cerebral hemispheres. A course of therapy usually involves six sessions. The shock produces a seizure and temporary memory loss. It is possible that this memory loss allows disordered thinking to be restructured. Alternative explanations are that the shock causes neurochemical changes, especially affecting noradrenaline, serotonin and dopamine transmission, all related to depression. It has also been suggested that ECT may act as a punishment and effect a cure in this way.

The second biological therapy is psychosurgery, a method rarely used because of its irreversible nature. It involves severing connections to parts of the brain in order to reduce abnormal behaviour. In the 1930s, many prefrontal lobotomies were performed where portions of the frontal cortex were removed to make aggressive patients more docile. There were many undesirable effects, such as reduced functioning and death. Prefrontal leukotomies involve more precise surgery, where needles are inserted to sever connections, effecting a functional lobotomy.

Stereotactic neurosurgery is still more precise; a system of precise coordinates is used to sever very specific connections using an electric current. Amygdalotomies result in disconnection of the amygdala and reduced anger and emotion. Cingulotomies (disconnecting the cingulate gyrus) are also performed to reduce anger.

The third and most common form of biological therapy is the use of drugs (chemotherapy). There are four main classes of drug: antidepressants, such as SSRIs (e.g. Prozac), which increase the activity of serotonin and thus reduce depression; antimanic drugs, such as lithium carbonate, which is used to treat manic depression; antipsychotic drugs, such as chlorpromazine, which is given to schizophrenics — such drugs block dopamine receptor sites; and, finally, anti-anxiety drugs, such as benzodiazepines (e.g. Valium), which generally lower activity in the nervous system and thereby reduce anxiety.

e In this answer, the candidate has managed to combine breadth (describing all three major biological therapies) with depth. There is a considerable amount of detail for each therapy, although it is somewhat list-like. The psychological content is accurate and there is a coherent structure and a clear range of synoptic links in terms of the variety of treatments covered. This is worth 13 marks out of 15.

(b) In order to determine the value of these therapies, we should consider their strengths and limitations.

The strengths are that they work. ECT is particularly effective with cases of severe depression where other forms of therapy have failed. Janicak et al. (1985) found that 85% of all depressed patients improved with ECT — a higher figure than for drug therapy.

Psychosurgery also has some supporters for its effectiveness. For example, Cosgrove et al. (1996) claimed successful treatment of depression using cingulo-tomies, but this support is rare.

Drug therapy is hugely popular possibly because, like all the biological thera-pies, the patient doesn't have to do anything, unlike psychotherapies which require thought and effort. Mental illnesses that appear to have a clear physical basis can be treated with drugs effectively. For example, depression is associated with a physical cause (low levels of serotonin) and antidepressants work well to restore the balance and alleviate the depression. Spiegel (1985) reports 65% effectiveness with tricyclics. Antipsychotic drugs can be used in conjunction with psychotherapy to form a more effective treatment programme.

Drugs have the advantage of being quick and accessible to all. However, there are many limitations. All drugs have side effects, such as blurred vision with antipsychotic drugs. There is also the problem of addiction (physically and/or psychologically). Once patients start taking a drug, they may be afraid to stop in case their symptoms return. A further issue is the idea that drugs are not a cure but a form of 'bandage' which gives the illusion of cure. It is difficult to assess their effectiveness in comparison with other therapies because the question of what constitutes 'relief' is a subjective one. Some clinicians and patients may use different criteria of effectiveness.

A further limitation concerns ethics. The prescription of drugs or other physical forms of therapy may infringe individual rights. In the case of psychosurgery, the treatment is irreversible, while the same effects may result from the other therapies as well. A patient may not wish to take medication but there is a balance between individual rights and those of society. A schizophrenic patient may be released from hospital but not take the prescribed drugs and be a danger to society. Drugs may be seen as a method of social control, but they are also a form of protection.

Biological methods take a determinist and reductionist approach, which has strengths and weaknesses. It reduces our understanding of mental illnesses to a rather simplistic view — that they can be treated like physical illnesses — and may deny the patient access to more insightful therapies which may offer a real cure. However, as suggested earlier, drug therapy may be used in conjunction with psychotherapy because it enables some disabling symptoms to be subdued so that the patient (e.g. someone very depressed or anxious) can begin to think about the problem. Perhaps it is best to take the view that biological therapies can be part of a more global system of therapy and are not ends in themselves. It is important for individuals and society at large to take this view.

🖉 This answer considers both strengths and weaknesses of all forms of biological therapy, and takes an informed approach by citing the findings of various studies. There is clear evidence of synopticity (e.g. the mention of ethics and determinism plus the contrasts made with other approaches). There is a slight flaw in that not all arguments are clearly explained (e.g. at the end of the fifth paragraph: 'Some clinicians and patients may use different criteria of effectiveness'), which omits coherent elaboration. This is the danger of trying to cover too much material. This essay scores 13 marks out of 15.

🖉 **The total awarded is 26 marks out of 30.**

Behavioural therapies

'Maladaptive behaviours are learned through classical and operant conditioning. They can be unlearned in the same way — at least that's what behavioural therapists believe.'

Discuss behavioural therapies, with reference to the issues raised in the quotation above.

(30 marks)

In a question that requires you to make reference to a quotation, marks will be lost if this is not done effectively and sustained throughout your essay (maximum AO2 marks if the quotation is not addressed are 9 out of 15). It is therefore important to grasp the meaning of the quotation and to use it to structure your essay. In the case here, the quotation directs you to consider (AO1) how conditioning theory can be used to explain the underlying assumptions of behavioural therapies: that is, describe the role of conditioning theory in learning and getting rid of (unlearning) maladaptive behaviours. You will also gain credit for describing the therapies themselves.

The quotation does not offer any direction about evaluation (AO2) but the injunction 'discuss' means that you should evaluate and comment on behavioural therapies as well as describe them. You might also evaluate the assumptions of behavioural therapies.

For full marks, you must discuss at least two therapies because the question asks for 'behavioural *therapies*'. If you consider only one therapy, a partial performance penalty will apply to AO1 and AO2.

■ ■ ■

Answer to question 8: B-grade candidate

The basic assumption of behavioural therapies is that all behaviour is learned and can be unlearned. Maladaptive behaviours are the same as any others. Behaviour is learned through classical conditioning, where a reflex response comes to be associated with a neutral stimulus so that a new stimulus–response link is formed. An example of this can be seen in the case of Little Albert, studied by Watson and Rayner. Albert was shown a white rat and had no fear. Then on several occasions when he was shown the rat he was also exposed to a loud noise which would create an innate fear response. After a number of trials, the sight of the rat alone made Albert jump and this generalised to other white furry things, such as Watson's beard. This experiment was unethical because it caused Albert distress and the experimenters were never able to uncondition him because his mother took him away. It is not clear how good an explanation of phobias this is because, for example, when people with phobias of dogs are interviewed they don't always report a bad experience with a dog. Perhaps they do not remember it. In addition, not everyone who is bitten by a dog develops a phobia.

Nevertheless, the principles of classical conditioning are used successfully to treat many phobias. In fact, behavioural therapy is one of the few ways to treat phobias. Systematic desensitisation is a form of classical conditioning where a patient learns to associate the feared thing with a new response, that is, relaxation. First, the patient learns how to relax. Next, the patient constructs a hierarchy of fearful things from least to most fearful. Then the patient is asked to imagine the least fearful thing while relaxing at the same time. It is not possible to experience two conflicting emotions simultaneously, so eventually the fear is replaced by relaxation and this conditioned response is paired with the feared stimulus. Then the patient imagines the next most fearful thing in the hierarchy and so on, until the fear is gone. If at any time the patient feels anxious, he/she is reminded to stop and regain composure and relaxation.

It is possible that systematic desensitisation works for reasons other than unlearning. For example, it can be explained in terms of cognitive restructuring, i.e. patients do not form new associations but change the way they think about the feared object. Any reference to thinking is beyond behaviourism. However, cognitive–behavioural therapy is a more recent development of behaviour therapy which combines elements of both.

There are other behavioural therapies based on classical conditioning as well as those based on operant conditioning. A successful example of the latter is token economy. If behaviours are learned because of rewards and reinforcers then the new, more desirable behaviours can be learned in this way. The principle of operant conditioning is that any behaviour that results in a pleasant state of affairs is more likely to be repeated. In the case of a person with maladaptive behaviours, these can be identified and only desirable behaviours are rewarded with tokens, which can then be exchanged for other things (e.g. sweets). This can be used in an institutional setting to teach patients to learn to make their beds and look after themselves, for example. It has also been used in the treatment of eating disorders.

The main problem appears to be that the new learned behaviours do not always transfer to life outside the institutions. This may be understood in terms of context-dependent learning, which suggests that we learn to do certain things in certain situations because of rewards specific to that situation, but the same S–R links do not transfer elsewhere.

It is possible to explain the success of token economies in ways other than through conditioning theory. It could be that the system allows for more careful structuring of the therapeutic situation and this leads to improvements. Recovery may also be due to a general increase in attention or even more emotional care from nursing staff. The therapy raises ethical concerns because behaviour manipulation is involved. Someone has to decide what constitutes a desirable behaviour (the one to be acquired) and what is undesirable.

There are general issues relating to evaluating a therapy, such as what constitutes a cure. Just removing certain symptoms, which is the goal of behaviour therapies, does not mean that a problem is solved. It may well be that an underlying problem remains and will soon be expressed through other symptoms. Behaviourists assume that there are no underlying behaviours that need concern us; there are only symptoms. If they are removed, then the patient is cured.

📝 The essay begins with a coherent but brief description of the assumptions of behavioural therapies, addressing the quotation. There are two further paragraphs credited as AO1, describing systematic desensitisation and token economies. Both descriptions are reasonably detailed (good depth) but overall AO1 is limited by the fact that only two therapies are covered. There is limited evidence of synopticity. This part of the answer is worth 8 marks out of 15. The candidate fares slightly better with AO2, making a number of evaluative points and relating these to the quotation (e.g. 'new behaviours that are learned don't always transfer...'). Ethical concerns are mentioned and some attempt is made to make links to other therapies, although, again, synopticity is limited. 9 marks out of 15 are awarded.

📝 **Overall, 17 marks out of a possible 30 are awarded.**

Alternatives to biological and behavioural therapies

Critically consider two or more therapies derived from either the psychodynamic or the cognitive–behavioural model of abnormality.   (30 marks)

The specification names both psychodynamic and cognitive–behavioural models of abnormality as alternatives to the biological and behavioural models. It is anticipated that candidates will study only one of these alternative models and questions will always be asked in such a way that you can use either model. In this essay, you may go for breadth, and cover several different therapies within the model, or depth, and cover only two therapies. Either route can lead you to full marks, although the former may offer a broader view of psychology (synopticity). You will not gain extra credit if you write about therapies derived from both models, unless you explicitly use one model as a form of evaluation. In fact, you will probably lose marks if you describe therapies derived from two models because you will have reduced the time available for each therapy.

Candidates who only cover one therapy would receive a maximum of 9 out of 15 for AO1 and for AO2. The lack of a second therapy also affects the synoptic content of the answer.

■ ■ ■

Answer to question 9: C-grade candidate

This essay will consider cognitive–behavioural therapies and evaluate their effectiveness. There are many cognitive–behavioural therapies. They are, in part, behavioural because they focus on changing observable behaviours, but they differ from behavioural therapies because they also believe that what needs to be changed is the way patients think about their problems, rather than the problems themselves. Cognitive–behavioural therapists believe that mental disorders are due to faulty thinking. This is a good way to approach psychological problems, but only those of a certain kind, such as depression or stress management. It is too simple for major disorders such as schizophrenia.

One example of a cognitive–behavioural therapy is Meichenbaum's stress inoculation therapy. This is used as a means of dealing with stress by getting prepared beforehand. People are taught by a therapist to make certain self-statements so that when they are in a stressful situation they can deal with it. This is a very good way to deal with stress because you learn to do it beforehand. It has been shown to be very successful.

Another cognitive–behavioural therapy is Beck's cognitive triad. This is a way of representing the depressed person's world. There are three cognitions that the depressed person holds — about him/herself, about the world and about the future.

The therapy aims to identify the self-defeating statements that the patient makes about any or all of these, and to challenge these statements so that the patient can see they don't hold up. This is called cognitive restructuring therapy and has been successful with depressed individuals and also people with eating disorders.

Another cognitive–behavioural therapy is Ellis's rational–emotional therapy. This uses the idea of ABC. There is first of all an activating event (A). The individual holds beliefs (B) about this event and these beliefs lead to consequences (C). The therapist identifies the beliefs and is aggressive in challenging them. This kind of directive and aggressive approach is quite different from counselling, where the therapist tries to be understanding, allowing the patient to become self-accepting. Rational–emotive therapy is quite threatening and you might think that it would make some people give up and not want to continue with the therapy. However, it appears to be quite successful. Maybe some people like to be challenged. It is possible that patients are just enjoying the attention from the therapist, even though it may seem to be negative. The increased attention could then explain the success of this therapy rather than the idea that the therapist is changing faulty cognitions.

Psychodynamic therapies also involve thinking, but they are quite different from cognitive–behavioural therapies. In Freud's psychoanalysis, patients talk to the therapist about anything that comes into their heads and this way they reveal their unconscious thoughts. The therapy is based on the belief that repressed thoughts lead to disturbed behaviour and the way to normality is by facing the unconscious thoughts. A psychoanalyst also analyses dreams and deals with transference.

There are other therapies too, such as ECT and drugs, which are used a lot. They are popular because they require little effort on the part of the patient, whereas cognitive–behavioural therapies mean that a patient has to work at getting better. Behavioural therapies are similar to cognitive–behavioural therapy but focus only on behaviour and not on altering thought. One behavioural therapy is aversion therapy, for example where a patient is given a drug that makes them sick when they drink alcohol and this makes them avoid drinking in the future.

Cognitive–behavioural therapies produce quick results and are very popular.

🖉 This candidate has offered reasonably detailed descriptions of three cognitive–behavioural therapies, although the first (Meichenbaum's stress inoculation method) is rather sketchy. This might be described as 'increasing breadth and depth'. The range is also important for synopticity which is otherwise lacking. The essay is coherent and well constructed. It is awarded 8 out of 15 AO1 marks. The AO2 material is less well developed, often making statements such as 'this is successful', with no further support. The material on other therapies has not been used effectively as evaluation and thus receives minimal credit (6 marks out of 15).

🖉 **A total of 14 marks out of 30 is awarded.**